# Walter Benjamin and the Bible

◆ ◆ ◆

BRIAN BRITT

*Walter Benjamin
and the Bible*

✦ ✦ ✦

CONTINUUM ✦ NEW YORK

1996

The Continuum Publishing Company
370 Lexington Avenue
New York, NY 10017

Copyright © 1996 by Brian Britt

Printed in the United States of America

Library of Congress Cataloging-in-Publication Data

Britt, Brian M., 1964–
    Walter Benjamin and the Bible / Brian Britt.
        p.      cm.
    Includes bibliographical references and index.
    ISBN 0-8264-0879-6 (alk. paper)
    1. Benjamin, Walter, 1892–1940—Religion.  2. Bible.  O.T.–
–Criticism, interpretation, etc.—History—20th century.  I. Title.
B3209.B58B75   1996
221—dc20                                          95-53723
                                                      CIP

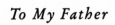

*To My Father*

# Contents

# Acknowledgments

$M$any people have supported my work on this project. I wish to thank the teachers and colleagues at the University of Chicago who first encouraged and assisted me in the study of Benjamin, especially Loren Kruger, Anthony Yu, Michael Fishbane, David Tracy, and Arnold Davidson. The National Foundation for Jewish Culture and Wesleyan College supported my research at several stages. Other friends and colleagues—Paul Mendes-Flohr, John Harkness, and Stephen Britt—read drafts and made helpful comments. Erin Miller read and proofread the manuscript, making valuable suggestions. My editor, Justus George Lawler, encouraged me to complete this project before I began, and he followed it with patience and care. Jessica Meltsner, my wife, advised me on many decisions about structure and content; she helped make the time I needed for its completion; and she, with my daughter Lucy, sustained me as I wrote.

# Introduction

*M*any studies of Walter Benjamin have concentrated on the role of religion or theology in his work. There are just as many books and essays about Benjamin's theory of language. The purpose of this book is related but different: to examine the category of sacred text in Benjamin's work. This study seeks to show that the idea of sacred text describes and connects the major stages of Benjamin's career. Because Benjamin seldom explicitly mentions sacred texts, it is easy to overlook the centrality of this concept to his work. But beneath this reticence is a persistent interest in the cultural influence of sacred texts, particularly the Bible.

One reason why the labels "theology," "mysticism," and "Marxism" prove inadequate to describe Benjamin's project is that they do not describe what he did; he was more of a writer and cultural critic than a theologian, mystic, or orthodox Marxist. He devoted himself to the study and composition of texts, some of which he considered to be repositories of the sacred. From his doctoral dissertation on the early romantics to the later studies of baroque allegory *(Trauerspiel)*, Kafka, and Baudelaire, Benjamin searched for modes and models of writing that reflected a notion of sacred text, one that I refer to as the archive of pure language. Benjamin reads Western culture as a succession of texts linked by a tradition of the sacred, but his goal is neither to write nor to gloss sacred texts.[1] Instead, Benjamin writes philosophical criticism of language, sacred texts, and modern culture.

## Biographical Overview

Benjamin's 1912 letters to Ludwig Strauss, outlining a position he called "cultural Zionism," paved the way for a fruitful intellectual career that would end in 1940 with a failed escape from the Nazis. Benjamin sought to practice an authentically Jewish and European cultural critique, but he found little support for this project, even among his close friends Gershom Scholem and Theodor Adorno. "Cultural Zionism" is neither theology nor politics, but it has elements of each.

Born in 1892 to a wealthy Jewish family in Berlin, Benjamin was educated at a "humanistic Gymnasium" and joined the youth movement led by the educational reformer Gustav von Wyneken.[2] Although he embraced the romantic humanism of German youth culture (rather than a Zionist youth group, for example), Benjamin took his Jewish identity seriously. Long before he met Gershom Scholem, Benjamin took an interest in Martin Buber's Jewish revival in Germany. In 1912, Benjamin formed a notion of himself as a Jewish intellectual whose task was to draw "from art Spirit for the life of the epoch"; in a letter from the same period, he describes a "cultural Zionism which sees Jewish values *everywhere* and works for them. Here I will stay, and I believe I must stay."[3]

Benjamin's study of literature and philosophy led to his doctoral dissertation on the early romantic notion of art in which he first sketches his own notion of critique. In the nineteen-twenties, his interests diverged; he translated Baudelaire's *Tableaux Parisiens;* wrote a study of German baroque tragedy *(Ursprung des deutschen Trauerspiels),* which he unsuccessfully submitted to complete his academic dossier; and he published a modernist book of aphorisms on urban culture called *One-Way Street.*

The book, dedicated to the Latvian revolutionary Asja Lacis, marks a shift toward Marxism for Benjamin, leading to associations with Theodor Adorno and Bertolt Brecht. Nevertheless, he considered dialectical materialism to be fundamentally theological.[4] From 1930 until his death ten years later, he wrote essays about contemporary art and literature and began an enormous project on nineteenth-century culture, the *Passagen-Werk.* Benjamin's literary and philosophical interests in language, experience, and texts, remained fundamentally unchanged.

## Sacred Text

The primary purpose of this book is to explicate the idea of sacred text in Benjamin's work. In opposition to traditions that privilege speech over writing, Benjamin consistently emphasized writing in his reflections on language. From at least 1916 onward, Benjamin posited an ideal language, the only access to which is found in texts, particularly sacred texts like the Bible. Sacred texts do not, however, provide a magical key to the recovery of pure language. Rather, they paradoxically gesture toward pure language through narratives of its loss. The paradox of sacred texts in Benjamin overlaps with the paradox of tradition (or, in John McCole's phrase, the "antinomies of tradition") and the paradox of messianism: the past determines but also eludes the present.

Benjamin does not differentiate sacred and secular texts a priori. While the Bible constitutes the prototypical sacred text, Benjamin finds the same principle at work in baroque allegory, Baudelaire, surrealism, and many other intellectual currents of the nineteenth and twentieth centuries. In his unfinished study of nineteenth-century Paris, the Arcades project, Benjamin characterizes buildings and commodities as "texts" that try unsuccessfully to recapture pure language.[5] But "sacred text" is not a category of objects so much as a cultural function. Instead of describing all these cultural expressions as sacred texts, it is more accurate to ascribe a quality to them, which I call the *scriptural function.*

The second purpose of this book is to suggest how the idea of sacred text can contribute to religious studies. Scholars frequently describe the Bible as a sacred text, but there have been almost no attempts to theorize or even to define this term. There are two commonly held views of sacred text: *externalist* notions, which regard a text's sacrality as constituted by external social and historical phenomena, and *internalist* notions, which claim a text is sacred on the basis of its contents. But this polarization of internalist and externalist theories reflects a false opposition. The Benjaminian idea of sacred text includes internalist and externalist elements without reducing one to the other.

This study also applies Benjamin's scriptural view of Western culture to the Bible itself. The end of Deuteronomy, which I treat here as a test case, incorporates a notion of sacred text that includes several layers and the suggestion that the *torah* is life.* In biblical

---

*In order to distinguish between biblical and postbiblical uses of the term, *torah* will refer to the Hebrew term as it appears in Deuteronomy, and "Torah" will apply to contemporary uses of the concept.

studies, the debate about sacred text has led to an impasse between historical–critical (usually externalist) and confessional (usually internalist) positions. Claims that the Bible is a sacred text raise the question, Sacred for whom? Some writers imply that the Bible can be seen as a sacred text only *within* religious communities.[6] Others, such as Michael Fishbane, suggest it is a sacred text for Western culture in general.[7] Fishbane sketches a "new type of sacredness" for the Bible: "not the sacredness of the raging, exclusive vision, but the sacredness of the chastened, inclusive one."[8] Such a view of the Bible as sacred text would stem not from sectarianism but would rather be "critical of the potential dangers of human symbolic systems, and an advocate for their fragility and plurality."[9] It is such a model of the Bible as sacred text that I develop.

Chapter 1 proposes a shift from the term sacred text to "scriptural function." A text exhibits the scriptural function if its content or context participate significantly in a religious or sacred tradition. Texts ranging from the Bible to contemporary literature come within the purview of the scriptural function. The chapter illustrates the scriptural function with an analysis of Deuteronomy 31–34.

The second chapter situates the concept of sacred text in the context of Benjamin's theory of language. According to Benjamin, language originally denotes objects mimetically; with the multiplicity of historical languages, however, objects become "overnamed" *(überbenannt),* and language thus becomes bourgeois and instrumentalized.[10]

In this fallen linguistic state (which corresponds to modernity) it is primarily the reading, translation, and criticism of texts that, however obliquely, point toward the restoration of pure language. Chapter 3 examines Benjamin's critical praxis as the attempt to evoke or recover pure language.

What is the status of the Bible in the modern world? Chapter 4 compares Benjamin's idea of the Bible to the work of Martin Buber and Franz Rosenzweig on the Bible and biblical translation. While Buber and Rosenzweig propose direct encounters with the text, Benjamin argues that moderns should first examine their own historical and epistemological relation to the Bible. The fifth chapter examines Benjamin's biblical interpretations and references.

Benjamin's final works, the Arcades project (the *Passagen-Werk*) and "On the Concept of History," developed a set of historical methods and categories.[11] For Benjamin, contemporary history represents the "document of barbarism" written by the brutal victor; and yet the philosopher is endowed with a "weak Messianic power" with which to counteract this barbarism.[12] Chapter 6 analyzes the role of the scriptural function in Benjamin's historiography and narratology, and the conclusion places the idea of the scriptural function in the context of religious studies, hermeneutics, and cultural studies.

## Methodological Note

There are many competing schools of Benjamin interpretation, ranging from the purely theological to the purely political and from those who construe Benjamin's work as solid, coherent philosophy to those who view it as incoherent obscurantism. The position taken here falls between these sets of extremes; on this view, Benjamin's earlier work on language, aesthetics, and baroque allegory shape the whole body of his work. The immediate concern of this book, Benjamin's notion of sacred text, is a central category in his early and late thought, linked closely to the early linguistic philosophy and to the later philosophy of history. It is therefore surprising that Benjamin scholars have almost completely ignored the category of sacred text. For Benjamin, sacred texts, especially the Bible, represent archives of lost pure language, which it is the task of philosophy to restore. As such, sacred texts, primarily the Bible, reveal the foundational nature of pure language. Benjamin explores the philosophical potential of sacred texts not so much through conventional exegesis as through a consideration of the cultural and conceptual legacy of the Bible, especially with respect to language.

Benjamin's writings do not form a coherent philosophical system. There is no single subject matter or terminology common to his major works. My argument that the notion of sacred text operates throughout Benjamin's career comes more from inference and comparison than from direct mentions of the term "sacred text." The diversity of Benjamin's writings, I suggest, reflects the variety of compositional modes, contexts, and areas in which he worked. Terms like "religion," "theology," "Judaism," and "the sacred" appear throughout his writings, but so does political language. This variety is a key to the category of sacred text: different cultural phenomena, from the Bible to allegory and modern art, belong to the same tradition. But Benjamin was reluctant to propose definite solutions to philosophical problems. His works show a preference for describing the problem, a compositional strategy I call the rhetoric of the task (chapter 3).

A word must also be said about interpreting Benjamin's writings. Because their meaning lies to a great extent in their juxtaposition of disparate elements, paraphrase and summary risk oversimplification. Critics of Benjamin tend either to reduce his work to a set of propositions without considering their manner of composition or to dismiss his work as obscurantist. In order to avoid such misrepresentations, interpretations of Benjamin's work must recognize how his original notions of language, text, and philosophy are put into practice in philosophical compositions.

### NOTES

1. The problematic terms "West" and "Western culture" are intended to limit, not privilege, the discussion. Benjamin identified himself as a European and wrote primarily about European culture.

2. *Gesammelte Schriften,* ed. Rolf Tiedemann and H. Schweppenhäuser (Frankfurt: Suhrkamp, 1991), 6: 216–17 (hereinafter cited as *GS)* and John McCole, *Walter Benjamin and the Antinomies of Tradition* (Ithaca: Cornell University Press, 1993), 35 ff.

3. Benjamin, letters to Ludwig Strauss, 11 September and 10 October 1912, cited in Rabinbach, "Between Enlightenment and Apocalypse," 95–96; the latter is published in *GS* 2: 836–38; both appear in *Benjaminiana,* ed. Hans Puttnies and Gary Smith (Giessen: Anabas, 1991), 46–52.

4. See "Über den Begriff der Geschichte," *GS* 1: 63.

5. See especially *Das Paris des Second Empire bei Baudelaire,* in *GS* 1: 511–604.

6. See Paul Ricoeur, "The 'Sacred' Text and the Community," in *The Critical Study of Sacred Texts,* ed. Wendy D. O'Flaherty (Berkeley: Berkeley Religious Studies Series, 1979), 271–76; and Jon Levenson, "The Eighth Principle of Judaism and the Literary Simultaneity of Scripture," *Journal of Religion* 68 (April 1988): 223–25.

7. J. Hillis Miller, "Tradition and Difference," *Diacritics* (Winter, 1972): 6–13. Michael Fishbane, "The Notion of Sacred Text," in *The Garments of Torah* (Bloomington: University of Indiana Press, 1989), 121–31.

8. Fishbane, *The Garments of Torah*, 131.

9. Ibid., 131.

10. Walter Benjamin, "On Language as Such and on the Language of Man," in *Reflections*, ed. Peter Demetz, trans. Edmund Jephcott (New York: Schocken Books, 1986), 330; *GS*, 2: 155.

11. These include the Baudelaireian *flâneur* and the aesthetic and critical category of *shock*, in which techniques such as montage can bring about a stoppage or momentary elevation in consciousness, or "dialectics at a standstill." See Susan Buck-Morss, *The Dialectics of Seeing* (Cambridge: MIT Press, 1989), 219.

12. Benjamin, "Theses on the Philosophy of History," in *Illuminations*, ed. Hannah Arendt, trans. Harry Zohn (New York: Schocken, 1969), 254–56.

CHAPTER 1

# Sacred Texts and
# the Scriptural Function

> My thinking relates to theology as blotting paper to ink: it is
> completely saturated with it. But if one were to go by the
> blotting paper, nothing written would remain.[1]

What is a sacred text? Somewhere along the boundaries of the
philosophy of religion, theology, and biblical studies, this question
has vanished from discussion. Even in theoretical treatments of
canon, hermeneutics, and the definition of religion, the subject of
sacred text is either avoided or taken for granted. Yet the category
of sacred text, especially as it refers to the Bible, informs and
underlies Western ideas of interpretation, law, and literature. This
chapter develops a concept of sacred text for Western biblical
culture—the scriptural function—and applies it to Deuteronomy
31–34, a reflexive and complex text that equates *torah* with life.
According to this concept, a text exhibits the scriptural function
if it participates significantly in a religious or sacred tradition.

As noted in the introduction, concepts of sacred text fall into two
polarized groups: *externalist* notions, which view a text's sacrality as
constituted by social and historical features, and *internalist* notions,
which claim a text is sacred on the basis of the text's content.
Externalist definitions view sacred text as a historically contingent
category having little connection to the text's origins or contents;
a text is sacred merely because a community says and believes it
to be so.[2] This view frequently appears in historical-critical biblical
studies. This approach risks cultural and epistemological nar-
rowness by focusing on the (usually conscious) beliefs of community members. It also treats sacred text only as a condition or

status, rather than as a dynamic hermeneutical process. Internalist accounts, on the other hand, tend to characterize the text as *necessarily* sacred based on its content, whether in terms of divine origin, moral teaching, or literary sublimity.[3] Most religious communities affirm the internalist view on the basis of divine authority, inspiration, or authorship.

Internalist and externalist views of sacred text take a definitional approach to the problem, seeking criteria to distinguish sacred from nonsacred texts. These approaches persist in contemporary biblical studies, where the impasse between externalist (historical-critical) and internalist (confessional) positions on the sacrality of the Bible remains unresolved by canonical criticism, for example, that of Brevard Childs.[4]

In contrast, the idea of sacred texts developed here concentrates on their function as well as their status. Texts may perform this "scriptural function" on internalist *and* externalist grounds in a variety of cultural contexts. The Bible models this view; its status as sacred text emerges from the testimony of its own internal claims and from the traditions that subsequently interpreted and affirmed them. Any discussion of the Bible's sacrality must therefore consider both biblical texts (and contexts) and the history of religious practice and exegesis that contributed to the Bible's contemporary status in Western culture. James Barr argues that the "[t]heological study of the Bible does take place in the context of the church; but that is not the only context that it has. It also has a context in a wider academic community."[5] The same problem is expressed by Gerhard Ebeling in "The Bible as a Document of the University":

> The Bible will always remain a highly important historical source, primarily of course for the history of religions, but also for the history of the ancient near East, for Semitic, Greek, and Latin philology. Yet far more significant is the enormous impact of the Bible upon all areas of our culture. Whether one studies philosophy or literature, history of art, music, psychology, or sociology, everywhere one encounters the Bible.[6]

Defining sacred text raises questions of criteria and boundaries: What's in and what's out? How religious or ritualized must a text be in order to count as a sacred text? The Apocrypha, midrashim, biblical commentary, religious poetry, and allegory present problem cases for any definition of sacred text. Walter Benjamin, though, develops an idea of sacred text that applies to most Western literature. Following Benjamin, this study proposes a notion of the *scriptural function*, which describes a *dimension* of texts that, through some combination of internal and external criteria, makes the text sacred. Like Roman Jakobson's idea of the poetic function, the notion of scriptural function shifts the question of sacred text from internal and external elements to participation or nonparticipation in a sacred or religious tradition.[7]

From its beginnings, biblical literature has developed through a dynamic of text and interpretation. As Michael Fishbane shows in *Biblical Interpretation in Ancient Israel*, the Hebrew Bible displays a complex network of intertextuality and interpretive processes. The Bible is inherently hermeneutical; instead of considering text to be primary and commentary secondary, it is more appropriate to view biblical literature as a combination of the two. No reading of Jeremiah is complete without Deuteronomy; no reading of Deuteronomy is complete without Genesis; no reading of Genesis is complete without Leviticus, and so on. It follows that the concept of sacred text must include interpretation, since interpretation *already exists* in the Bible. Accordingly, the scriptural function entails an interpretive process, especially one that makes the text's sacred status explicit through an identifiable tradition of canonization.

## The Philosophy of Walter Benjamin

Walter Benjamin's account of the Bible as sacred text includes internalist and externalist elements without reducing one to the other. Externalist analysis does not, for Benjamin, deny an internally sacred status for many religious communities and contemporary culture in general:

> Commentary and translation stand in the same relation to the text as style and mimesis to nature: the same phenomenon considered from different aspects. On the tree of the sacred

> text both are only the eternally rustling leaves *(Blätter)*; on that
> of the profane, the seasonally falling fruits.[8]

In the first sentence of this passage, scholarly work in the realm of texts is compared to artistic representations of nature. Benjamin compares text and nature through the human activities upon which they are based. The second sentence introduces a new opposition, the trees of the sacred and profane texts. By speaking of the two texts as trees, Benjamin collapses the previous text/nature opposition and evokes the two trees in Eden from Genesis 2–3. On the tree of the (biblical) sacred text, commentary and translation are leaves, but on the tree of the profane text commentary and translation are fruits.[9]

The heading over this passage reads, "These Plantings Have Been Entrusted to the Care of the Public."[10] The trees of sacred and profane texts require both that people avoid damaging them and that the trees be provided with the care they need to thrive. Like the two trees in the garden of Eden, the trees of the sacred and profane texts are accompanied by an injunction; like the garden, the plantings are entrusted to human care. This allusion, however, only serves to underscore the difference between the modern context, in which language and nature are degraded to the point at which a sign must be placed in front of plantings for their protection, and the Edenic context, in which nature and language flourish.[11]

In characteristically aphoristic fashion, Benjamin constructs a rich set of analogies, oppositions, and relations. If commentary and translation form leaves *(Blätter* also denotes pages) on the tree of the sacred text, then they constitute its necessary life and substance.[12] On the other hand, the image of commentary and translation as fruits on the tree of the profane text represents something more substantial both as produce and as potential for new trees. According to this view, what makes a text sacred is its reliance upon translation and commentary for vitality, but simultaneously and in contrast to profane texts, these leaves have no life or potential for life independent of the sacred text itself.

The dependence of the sacred text on commentary and translation for its vitality suggests an externalist notion of sacred text. At the same time, since the leaves have life only as part of the sacred text, Benjamin rules out a *merely* externalist position; a biblical commentary or translation on its own cannot confer life on the sacred text. In anticipation of reception and poststructuralist theory, Benjamin views a text as a constellation of discourses that posits some idea.[13] In other words, practices like translation, criticism, and commentary partly constitute the text.

This is as close as Benjamin comes to articulating the criteria that make a text sacred. In fact, it would be impossible to state these criteria more precisely, because our language and thought are degraded and fallen. From "The Task of the Translator" we can infer that message *(Mitteilung)* does not make a text sacred. Neither can the origin of a text, in a simple chronological sense, make it sacred.[14] His main concern is not to distinguish between sacred and profane texts but to describe a quality, which I call the scriptural function, that appears in many texts in many ways.

In Benjamin's linguistic philosophy, language has become the archive of the lost mimetic faculty, an arbitrary system of signs in place of an innate system of names.[15] The task of philosophy and criticism is to retrieve mimetic or pure language, which only becomes possible through sacred texts, the archives of pure language.[16] But this task can never be fully accomplished; the divine word preserved in the written text offers only a glimpse of pure language.

Sacred texts mediate the lost mimetic function of language and its current degraded condition. It is thus surprising that Benjamin scholars have almost completely ignored the category of sacred text. "The Bible," he writes, "in regarding itself as a revelation, must necessarily evolve the fundamental linguistic facts."[17]

Sacred texts constitute the archive of pure language through the interplay of text and commentary; the text functions as a canon, a status reinforced by the commentary. Benjamin explains this dynamic in *The Origin of German Tragic Drama:*

> The sanctity of what is written is inextricably bound up with the idea of its strict codification. For sacred script always takes the form of certain complexes (or systems: *Komplex*) of words which ultimately constitute, or aspire to become, one single and inalterable complex. So it is that alphabetical script, as a combination of atoms of writing, is the farthest removed from the script of sacred complexes. These latter take the form of

hieroglyphics. The desire to guarantee the sacred character of any script—there will always be a conflict between sacred standing (*sacraler Geltung*) and profane comprehensibility—leads to complexes, to hieroglyphics.[18]

The status of the text—its sacred standing—requires codification, even at the cost of being understood. By this account, the Bible itself is far removed from the highest order of sacred texts, because it is written alphabetically and often understandably. What any interpretation (whether translation or commentary) needs is a text, a tangible verbal artifact, as well as the ambiguity to open up a space in which to interpret. This interpretation, in turn, becomes a necessary component of the sacred text. Sacred texts require and guide interpretation.

The dynamic of original and subsequent commentary and translation constitutes sacred texts. At the same time, sacred texts posit an earlier, lost pure language. Thus, the original sacred text always points in two directions, a *traditum* in the context of a *traditio*.[19]

## The Scriptural Function

Since interpretation of different kinds lies at the heart of the sacred text,[20] interpretive practices such as translation and commentary mark a series of stages in the life of the text.[21] This suggests a paradox: the farther one gets from the historical origins of a text, the closer one gets to its sacred "origins." The idea of a life cycle for sacred texts also calls for a shift from the noun—sacred text—to an adjective—sacrality—or better, scriptural function. Scriptural function, like Jakobson's poetic function, denotes a dynamic quality of texts that make a religious claim on a community. In the West, the scriptural function obtains when a text takes part in the tradition of the Bible or biblical discourse; in Benjamin's terms, such a text becomes an archive of pure language.[22]

Definitions of sacred text depend on an internal feature such as its origin or on an external factor like community belief; these definitions divide all texts sharply into sacred and nonsacred groupings. The scriptural function, by contrast, enables us to conceive of allegory, theology, and commentary as part of the constellation of sacred text. The scriptural function even describes texts that are not ostensibly religious, because the standard criteria for sacrality—internal status or external function—no longer apply. Whole fields of discourse—modernist aesthetics, Marxist theory, and jurisprudence, to name three identified by Benjamin—depend on, derive from, or participate in the concept of sacred text proposed here.

Biblical culture—a term that arguably describes a great deal of Western tradition—could be diagrammed as a very elaborate constellation of interconnected discourses with the Bible at the center, serving as a model of both canon and canonization, text and commentary, or, in Michael Fishbane's terms, *traditum* and *traditio*. For Benjamin, allegory and abstraction disperse the Bible among other texts and concepts. Interpretive methods and concepts from the Bible obtain in the fields of literary studies and law, but they subsequently return to the Bible in a different (perhaps more rationalized) form and reshape its reception. From this standpoint, the Bible and biblical interpretation become indistinguishable, which is the reason Benjamin argues that contemporary perspectives and allegorical transformations must be analyzed before studying the Bible itself. Concerned more with mode than with meaning in texts (as in the essay on translation), Benjamin wrote almost no biblical commentary but did write hundreds of pages on the allegorical transformations of the Bible.[23]

## The Scriptural Function in Deut. 31–34

The concept of scriptural function does, however, apply to the Bible. A rich and representative example can be found in Deuteronomy 31–34, in which the subject of sacred text follows a trajectory from the text itself to all of Deuteronomy, the Pentateuch, and the entire Bible, and continues into the religious traditions of Judaism, Christianity, and Islam. The Bible contains hermeneutical models from the past and accommodates the perspectives of the future. In Deuteronomy 31–34, textual reflexivity and variety illustrate the scriptural function.

In Deuteronomy 31–34, Moses finishes reciting the divine laws that occupy most of the book and announces his death. The uninterrupted speech of Moses gives way to a narrative of his final actions, including the commission of Joshua as successor and the writing of the law and a Song (to be preserved as a witness for God against the people, 31:19–26). Moses recites two poetic texts, a didactic Song about the relation between God and Israel, and a blessing upon the tribes of Israel (an obvious parallel to Genesis 49). The poetic texts probably antedate the composition of the narrative and thus involve a kind of intratextual canonization. In 34:10–12, the narrative takes on an uncharacteristically direct tone in extolling the uniqueness of Moses.

In Deuteronomy 31–34, the death of Moses is associated with the writing of sacred texts and the command to preserve and recite them. The narrative, legal, and poetic texts gain legitimacy and authority through their Mosaic origin, serving both as a negative reminder to keep the law[24] and as a positive catalyst for community identity and tradition. Deuteronomy 31–34 thus raises the issue of sacred text through explicit reference to the writing, enshrinement, and ritual recitation of the laws and the song.

Ambiguities of chronology and agency in Deuteronomy 31–34 focus attention on the inscription of the *torah* and Song. The chain of events in chapter 31 is as follows. First, Moses announces his impending death and commissions Joshua as his successor (31:1–8). He then writes down "this *torah*," giving it to the Levites with instructions for its ritual recitation (vv. 9–13). In vv. 14–23, YHWH tells Moses to present himself with Joshua in the tent of meeting; then, after appearing to them in a pillar of cloud, YHWH commands Moses to write down and teach the Israelites a Song that will act as a witness against them after they become unfaithful. Moses obeys, and YHWH commissions Joshua directly.

The text then returns to the scene of Moses writing the *torah*, followed by a speech by Moses echoing that of YHWH in 16–21 admonishing the Israelites to use the written *torah* as a witness against their future infidelity (vv. 24–29). The instructions here differ from those in 9–13, and it is unclear whether the antecedent of "this *torah*" coincides with that of the earlier passage or with that of the Song mentioned just before. The first uninterrupted narrative concludes (in v. 30) with Moses reciting "this Song" to the Israelites. As this brief synopsis makes clear, the narrative of Deuteronomy 31 raises questions about the reference of *"torah"* and "Song," and about the chronology of the passage itself. Do the two texts and two sets of instructions overlap or follow one another? Moses writes the *torah,* then YHWH tells him to write the Song (which he does), then Moses finishes writing the *torah,* whereupon he recites the Song.

The exact identity of these writings remains unclear, which suggests a broader reference for *torah* than the Deuteronomic code. Tradition has taken this ambiguity to mean that Moses wrote Deuteronomy itself. The variety of texts in Deuteronomy 31–34 certainly suggests an inclusive concept of sacred text. If Moses' inscription of the *torah* optimistically points toward Israel's understanding and performance of the commandments, then the Song he recites will aim more modestly at witnessing against the people. Like the *torah,* the Song will be written and taught to the people, and it will even be put into their mouths, but the Song will not lead the people to fear YHWH and keep the *torah.* In the encouraging prediction about the text of the *torah,* Moses is the speaker; the contrasting resignation about the text of the Song comes from YHWH. Moses assures the people and Joshua that YHWH will not abandon or forsake them (vv. 6, 8), but YHWH complains that the Israelites will abandon and break his covenant with them (v. 16).

Writing thus has two functions in Deuteronomy 31: it can either bring about certain attitudes and behaviors in people or it can function as a witness (*'ed,* from *'ud,* "return" or "repeat," hence also reminder) against Israel that will not be forgotten even by future generations. Both texts will be learned (*lamad*) and remembered by the people, but only the *torah* will have the additional capacity to promote certain attitudes and behaviors, while the less efficacious Song perseveres in the people's memory but has no power over their actions. This contrast may derive in part from the content of the respective texts and in part from the attitudes of the speakers (optimistic Moses and pessimistic but omniscient YHWH). On the other hand, the two views of writing may represent fundamental differences in the understanding of written language and sacred text in Deuteronomy. Likewise, the juxtaposition of Song and Blessing with the narrative yields meaningful elements of a concept of sacred text. Their incorporation into the "canon" of Deuteronomy 31–34 projects a concept of sacred text that combines hermeneutical process with textual product. The seams between the poetic texts and their narrative context display the process of how the entire text is composed. At the same time, the poetic texts themselves contribute to the notion of sacred text: the Song constitutes a *mise en abîme* of the Mosaic covenantal tradition, with echoes of earlier warrior-god material, and the Blessing directly recalls Jacob's blessing in Genesis 49. While the Song and Blessing interrupt the narrative flow of Moses' farewell speech and death, thematically they reinforce the covenantal and textual concerns of Deuteronomy 31–34. Close analysis of this text reveals many layers and kinds of sacred texts; "scriptural function" describes the Bible even better than "sacred text."

## Torah as Life

Deuteronomy 31–34 broadens the reference of the term *torah* to include parenetic, poetic, and narrative discourse within and beyond Deuteronomy, ultimately into the rest of the biblical canon. The text displays a dialectic of closure and openness that resists reductionistic interpretations.[25] And while the Deuteronomic notion of sacred text aims at a particular religious community, its broadening impulse creates an open field of interpretive opportunities and yields the astonishing identification, also made by Benjamin, of Torah with life:

> Lay to heart all the words which I enjoin upon you this day, that you may commend them to your children, that they may be careful to do all the words of this law. For it is no trifle for you, but it is your life, and thereby you shall live long in the land which you are crossing the Jordan to possess. (Deut. 32:46–47)

Benjamin's equation of life with the Torah appears in a letter on Kafka. Kafka's writing contains, in his view, revelatory and messianic components: "That I do not deny the component of revelation in Kafka's work already follows from my appreciation—by declaring his work to be 'distorted' [*entstellt*]—of its messianic aspect."[26] The letter continues:

For the work of the Torah—if we abide by Kafka's account—has been thwarted *(vereitelt)*. It is in this context that the problem of the Scripture *(Schrift)* poses itself. Whether the pupils have lost it or whether they are unable to decipher *(enträtseln)* it comes down to the same thing, because, without the key that belongs to it, the Scripture is not Scripture, but life. Life as it is lived in the village at the foot of the hill on which the castle is built. It is in the attempt to metamorphose life into Scripture that I perceive the meaning of "reversal" *(Umkehr)*, which so many of Kafka's parables endeavor to bring about.[27]

In Kafka as in Deuteronomy 32, Torah becomes life. But ironically, Kafka's Torah becomes life only when it is thwarted. Whereas Deuteronomy enjoins Israel to a life of Torah, Benjamin's Kafka laments a Torah reduced to life, while hoping to reelevate life back to Torah. Such a reversal would require the ability to understand the coded system *(Komplex)* of the sacred text. In the world of Kafka's fiction, the thwarted sacred text becomes life while life aspires to become sacred text.

For Benjamin, the Bible has the status of sacred text in contemporary Western culture as an archive of pure language. The Bible and its tradition, which includes baroque allegory and Kafka's narratives, bear the traces of pure language as well as the narrative of its loss. Through compositional experimentation and epistemological speculation, Benjamin sets his own writing and translation to the task of restoring pure language. But instead of analyzing the Bible directly, he first analyzes his hermeneutical situation as the estrangement from the biblical paradise of pure language. Benjamin's writings gesture toward the restoration of pure language without ignoring the obstacles that lie in its way.

Both Benjamin and Deuteronomy display a variety of interpretive methods within the boundaries of the interpreted text. Both effectively collapse the dichotomies of closure and openness, sacred and profane, writing and life, progressing from Moses to *torah* and from spoken pure language (by Adam, the "first philosopher") to written sacred text. In Deuteronomy, sacred text includes both a witnessing of artifact *('ed)* and an ongoing interpretive process *(torah)* that becomes life itself. The same dynamic appears in Benja-

min's view that includes both sacred standing and profane comprehensibility. As artifact, the sacred text has boundaries; but as
interpretive process, sacred text is an ongoing activity that includes
(and even requires) commentary and translation. Because the recovery of pure language is always an incomplete task, sacred text refers
to the whole culture of interpretation proceeding from the Bible.
The equations of *torah* with life in Deuteronomy 32:47 and in
Benjamin's writings attend to the wealth of cultural activity sur-
rounding the sacred text of the Bible.

By incorporating its own hermeneutical models, Deuteronomy
31–34 overcomes the definitional and static approach of internalist
and externalist views. Biblical interpretation no longer refers to an
activity imposed on the passive text; rather, the biblical text guides
interpretation according to the hermeneutical models it incorporates. As both *traditum* and *traditio,* the sacred text of Deuteronomy
31–34 contains a hermeneutical blueprint for its own interpretation.

The hermeneutical models in Deuteronomy 31–34 include intratextual canonization, the use of ambiguity and juxtaposition to
broaden reference, and the models of sacred text as witnessing
artifact, life-altering instruction, and finally life itself.[28] Benjamin's
compositional techniques, including aphorism, montage, quotation,
and the rhetoric of the task, exhibit strikingly similar elements:
reflexivity, diversity of genres, and the dissolution of the dichotomies of openness and closure, transcendence and comprehensibility,
text and life. The sacred text of ancient Israel broadens the reference
of *torah* to include several genres and life itself; Benjamin's model
broadens the reference further to include the Bible as a basis of
Western linguistic thought as well as allegories, poetry, and narratives in the biblical tradition. The sacred text of the Bible contains
hermeneutical models from the past and accommodates the hermeneutical perspectives of the future. The scriptural function provides
a way for scholars of religion to talk about sacred texts outside
denominational boundaries and without retreating into internalist
or externalist definitions. A text exhibits the scriptural function if
its content or context participates significantly in a religious or
sacred tradition.[29] The scriptural function focuses on interpreting,
reciting, and preserving a religious tradition in writing. The analysis
of sacred texts reveals not monolithic complexes but rather complex

sites of interpretation. Deuteronomy 31–34, for example, illustrates the textual variety and reflexivity of the scriptural function. For Walter Benjamin, the scriptural function points toward an unattainable pure language; the task of the critic and translator is to identify and illuminate the scriptural function in texts and discourses. The following chapter traces Benjamin's view of sacred text to his theory of language.

NOTES

1. *GS* 5: 588.

2. A classic example is Max Weber's conception of the Bible in *The Protestant Ethic and the Spirit of Capitalism*, trans. Talcott Parsons (London: Unwin, 1930).

3. A recent version of this position appears in Northrop Frye's *The Great Code: The Bible and Literature* (New York: Harcourt Brace Jovanovich, 1982), esp. xiii–xix. See also Samuel Taylor Coleridge, *Confessions of an Inquiring Spirit* (Philadelphia: Fortress, 1988).

4. The only justification Childs provides for the study of the canonical text is theological. See the discussion in chapter 3, below.

5. James Barr, "Does Biblical Study Still Belong to Theology?" *The Scope and Authority of the Bible* (Philadelphia: Westminster, 1980), 29. Barr nevertheless limits his claims to the Bible's authority to "within the church" in an essay in the same collection, "Has the Bible any Authority?", 64.

6. Gerhard Ebeling, "The Bible as a Document of the University," in *The Bible as a Document of the University*, ed. Hans Dieter Betz (Chico, CA: Scholars Press, 1979), 14. Ebeling adds that the Bible might aid the contemporary crises of unity, freedom, and truth in the university because "in this book life as it is lived by people has become manifest in an enormous condensation, so much so that from it time and again new impulses for life as it is lived emerge," 18.

7. Roman Jakobson, "Linguistics and Poetics," in *The Structuralists: From Marx to Lévi-Strauss*, Richard T. and Fernande M. de George, eds. (Garden City, New York: Anchor, 1972), 93.

8. Walter Benjamin, "One-Way Street," in *Reflections*, 68; *Einbahnstrasse* (Frankfurt: Suhrkamp, 1991), 20.

9. See the discussion of Benjamin's analysis of Genesis in the essay on language and the reference to the tree of knowledge in the "Critique of Violence" below in chapter 2.

10. *Einbahnstrasse*, 20.

11. One consequence of the linguistic Fall in "On Language" is that, in a phrase echoing Hosea 4:3 and Joel 1:10, "nature mourns" ("On Language," in *Reflections*, 329).

12. Note the distinction between critique and commentary in the 1922 study of Goethe's *Wahlverwandtschaften*: "Die Kritik sucht den Wahrheitsgehalt eines

Kunstwerks, der Kommentar seinen Sachgehalt," *GS,* 1: 125. See also the discussion of "The Task of the Translator" in chapter 2.

13. See *GS* 1: 62–79; 4: 9–19, and McCole, 99–101.

14. See *GS* 1: 225–27.

15. *GS* 2: 210–13.

16. *GS* 4: 9, ff.

17. "On Language," in *Reflections,* 322.

18. Benjamin, *The Origin of German Tragic Drama,* trans. John Osborne (London: NLB, 1977), 175; *GS* 1: 351.

19. See Michael Fishbane, *Biblical Interpretation in Ancient Israel* (Oxford: Oxford University Press, 1989), 74–77.

20. Despite criticisms that the model of the text has become too dominant in religious studies [see Lawrence E. Sullivan, "'Seeking an End to the Primary Text' or 'Putting an End to the Text as Primary,'" in *Beyond the Classics?,* ed. Frank Reynolds and Sheryl Burkhalter (Atlanta: Scholars Press, 1990), 41–59], it remains to be seen whether there is a clear alternative to the model of the text for interpreters of textual as well as nontextual religious phenomena.

21. *GS* 4: 10–11.

22. This notion is developed in chapter 2.

23. Chapter 4 examines Benjamin's rare citations and interpretations of the Bible.

24. "For I know your rebelliousness and your stubbornness (stiffness of neck); behold, while I am yet alive with you, today you have been rebellious against YHWH; how much more after my death!" (31:27).

25. Fishbane suggests that the "capacity of the Bible to incorporate multiple structures of reality" may constitute a dimension of its sacrality (*The Garments of Torah,* 130–31).

26. Benjamin, Letter to Scholem, August 11, 1934, in *The Correspondence of Walter Benjamin and Gershom Scholem,* (New York: Schocken, 1989), 135; Benjamin, *Briefe,* Gershom Scholem and Theodor Adorno, eds. (Frankfurt: Suhrkamp Verlag, 1966), 618.

27. Ibid.

28. See Hans-Georg Gadamer, *Truth and Method: Second Revised Edition* (New York: Continuum, 1988), 250–51.

29. Of course, this definition depends on a concept of religion or the sacred, but there are several models, especially those of Geertz, Berger, Eliade, or Otto, that would suffice. The other main limitation of the scriptural function is its bias toward Western religious traditions, especially Judaism, Christianity, and Islam. On the other hand, religious studies as a field has historically maintained this bias at an unexamined level; one could argue the concept of sacred text is inherently culture-bound and ethnocentric.

CHAPTER 2

# Archive of Pure Language: Language and Sacred Text in Benjamin's Philosophy

> Yet I still need a closer definition of what I understand by fruitful cultural Judaism. . . . At base I have more of a picture of it than a line of thinking.
>
> It is the inverted building of the tower of Babel: the people of the Bible heap stone upon stone, and what is spiritually desired—the sky-towering tower does not emerge.
>
> The Jews handle ideas like stones, and the source, the matter, is never reached. They build from above without touching the ground.
>
> It formed a Christ in a Jewish woman: Hebbel "Judith" also "Herodes and Mariamne."[1]

The Bible is the last place most philosophers would look for a theory of language, and biblical scholars rarely undertake philosophy about the Bible.[2] Yet Walter Benjamin's writings on language deliberately seek this synthesis. The 1916 essay "On Language as Such and of the Language of Man" says as much about the Bible as it does about language. "The Bible," wrote Benjamin, "in regarding itself as a revelation, must necessarily evolve the fundamental linguistic facts *(die sprachlichen Grundtatsachen)*."[3]

Theodor Adorno characterizes Benjamin's idea of sacred text as follows:

> In any case, his notion of the sacred text was derived from the cabbala. For him philosophy consisted essentially in commentary and criticism, and language as a crystallization of the

"name," took priority over its function as bearer of meaning and even of expression. . . . He transposed the idea of the sacred text into the sphere of enlightenment, into which, according to Scholem, Jewish mysticism itself tends to culminate dialectically. His "essayism" consists in treating profane texts as though they were sacred. This does not mean that he clung to theological relics or, as the religious socialists, endowed the profane with transcendent significance. Rather, he looked to radical, defenceless profanation as the only chance for the theological heritage which squandered itself in profanity.[4]

Although he grasps the fundamental impetus of Benjamin's philosophy, Adorno misunderstands Benjamin's revision of the sacred-profane distinction, in which the sacred is not simply the reverse of the profane but an archive of pure language. Rather than imposing standard notions of the sacred on ostensibly profane texts, Benjamin demonstrates the relation of all texts to a nearly extinct model of language as self-communicating spiritual being.[5] It is inaccurate to suggest that Benjamin transposed sacred texts onto the enlightenment, since he claims that philosophy (e.g., Kant's notion of experience) overlooks its dependence on sacred texts. The task of philosophy, as outlined in the *Trauerspiel* study, is to represent and restore pure language through the conceptual analysis of sacred texts (in this case, allegory). The paradox of this view is that sacred texts are both elusive and fundamental to understanding.

The following analysis views Benjamin's works in a literary and philosophical light, as carefully wrought compositions whose meaning emerges not only from what they say but also from how they say it.[6] In fact, the compositional analysis reveals significant affinities between the notion of sacred text and Benjamin's writing.

## "On Language as Such and on the Language of Man" (1916)

In 1916, the same year in which he wrote to Martin Buber objecting to the view of language as a "pure means" to action, Benjamin wrote "Über Sprache überhaupt und über die Sprache des Menschen."[7] The essay's first part develops an ideal philosophical conception of language in the tradition of Hamann and Humboldt, and then expands it through an interpretation of Genesis 1–4 and 11. Although prefaced as a mere illustration, the biblical analysis lies at the center of the essay. In effect, Benjamin moves from the philosophical paradox of the relation between language and being to the concept of revelation, especially in the sacred text of the Bible.

Benjamin defines language as "all communication of spiritual meanings *(geistige Inhalte).*"[8] To this formulation he appends theological accounts of revelation, naming, and the origins of language based on the book of Genesis. Human language appears in its highest form as the completion and mirroring of the divine language of creation. By the middle of the essay, it becomes clear that Benjamin's concept of language opposes the standard view of language as a means of communication. In fact, his entire theory of language depends on and emerges from a notion of revelation typified by the Bible.

Key elements of the essay—the discussion of language in general, a connection between language and thought, and a theory of linguistic development—reveal the influence of the linguistic philosopher Wilhelm von Humboldt (1767–1835). Humboldt's work combines the impulse of German romanticism to find essential links between word, thought, and object, with the philological impulse to recognize conventionality and variability in languages.

But Benjamin has fundamental disagreements with Humboldt's views on language and culture.[9] For Humboldt, language is the direct and reliable expression of human thought.[10] We communicate thought through language. In his essays on language and translation, Benjamin rewrites the previous sentence in two ways, by replacing the human subject with "language" and "thought" with the Humboldtian term "spiritual being"; thus: "Language communicates its corresponding spiritual being." In a second revision of the statement, Benjamin replaces "language" with "spiritual being" and the preposition "through" to "in"; thus: "Spiritual being communicates itself *in* language and not *through* language."[11] Not only does Humboldt see language as the transparent complement of thought; language also constitutes the primary expression of human individuality and freedom.

Humboldt's terms—*das Mittel, zeigen, die Sprache überhaupt, das Wesen, der Ausdruck,* and *die Form*—are also Benjamin's terms. Some of their views also overlap: both insist on the immediacy of language and the possibility of speaking about language in general. The main area of difference lies in the reference and application of the linguistics. Humboldt sees language as a fundamental human capacity for free, individual expression within a national-linguistic system. Benjamin, on the other hand, departs from Humboldt's nationalism and changes the reference of "language" itself.

For Humboldt, language is a force for acculturation; the developmental condition of a nation's language contributes to the individual's freedom and creativity *(Bildung)* through the basic creative conception *(Bild)* of a language. This dynamic of the free self working within the confines of a particular national and linguistic *Bildung* is not fully addressed by Humboldt, although he considers inflected languages like Sanskrit to be more conducive to freedom, because of their grammatical flexibility, than noninflected languages like Chinese.[12] Despite his relative open-mindedness, Humboldt has difficulty avoiding racism.[13] For Benjamin the purpose of language is not socialization or even communication, as with Humboldt; on the contrary, it is a destabilizing force with transformative potential.

Instead of defining language as the expression of thought, Benjamin calls it the communication of the spiritual contents *(geistige Inhalte)* of things or people. Language expresses not the thought of an individual speaker but rather the spiritual essence of the language itself:

> Every language communicates itself *in* itself; it is in the purest sense the "medium" *(das Medium)* of the communication. Mediation *(das Mediale)*, which is the immediacy *(Unmittelbarkeit)* of all spiritual communication *(Mitteilung)*, is the fundamental problem of linguistic theory, and if one chooses to call this immediacy magic, then the primary problem of language is its magic. At the same time, the notion of the magic of language points to something else: its infiniteness. This is conditional on its immediacy.[14]

The paradox that mediation is the immediacy of communication constitutes the magic of language: this is evident in the language essay and later in a 1925 fragment criticizing Humboldt, and it poses an alternative to the idea of language as mere communication.[15] But this magic is not just mystification, as some scholars have suggested; rather, it serves as a kind of shorthand for an alternative—the pure language of naming—that is unavailable to contemporary language and experience.

The mention of magic as a synonym for the immediacy of language is central to Benjamin's argument.[16] The equation suggests that the same linguistic phenomena can be viewed from a rational, philosophical standpoint or from an "irrational," magical one; this maneuver reflects Benjamin's deeper conviction that linguistic philosophy coincides with metaphysical and religious thought. Magic also suggests to Benjamin that language is infinite, for "just because nothing is communicated *through* language, what is communicated *in* language cannot be externally limited or measured."[17] To explain this claim, Benjamin takes up a discussion of the most properly human form of language: naming.[18]

Far from being a way to communicate meaning, language communicates itself in itself, a phenomenon epitomized by naming: "Naming is that by which nothing beyond it is communicated, and *in* which language itself communicates itself absolutely."[19] Naming constitutes the core of human and divine language: *"It is therefore the linguistic being of man,"* he writes, *"to name things";*[20] "[I]n naming the spiritual being of man communicates itself to God."[21] With this, Benjamin turns standard ideas of language and mimesis on their heads. Instead of symbolizing something else, language expresses itself, and instead of linking word and object, "naming" links God and humanity. This "pure language" of naming has nothing to do with meanings; it communicates only itself. It is only after the Fall, when languages multiply, that words become "mere signs" and things become "overnamed" *(überbenannt).*[22] The mimesis of pure language relates human to God, not word to object.

Like Humboldt, Benjamin sees language as an expression of thought, but he radicalizes both terms, so that "language" denotes not so much actual languages as "spiritual being" *(geistige Wesen)* and a mimetic language of naming that precedes historical languages.

Thought, too, is defined broadly as spiritual being and spiritual contents *(geistige Inhalte)*; this is not only subjective cognition but also the independent contents of revelation. The language of naming, Benjamin contends, "knows no means *(Mittel)*, no object, and no addressee of communication."[23] This view revises the romantic notion of language in favor of a pure, mimetic language of naming and revelation that both underlies and remains hidden from contemporary experience.[24] It is precisely the banishment from this pure language, suggests Benjamin, that leads to the status of language as means, rational judgment, and abstraction.[25]

The essay becomes explicitly theological at this point. The term "the name" *(der Name)* begins four sentences in as many paragraphs, indicating not just "names" or "naming" but rather "the name," perhaps even alluding to the name of God.[26] Acknowledging the shift to the metaphysical plane, Benjamin introduces the term revelation *(Offenbarung)*. In contrast to the conventional view that revelation defies expression, Benjamin, because he identifies linguistic being with spiritual being, claims the opposite: "The highest spiritual region of religion is (in the concept of revelation) at the same time the only one that does not know the inexpressible. For it is addressed in name and expresses itself as revelation."[27]

The sentence states a double paradox: first, language properly communicates only its own spiritual being; second, in the case of revelation, language expresses itself as name without inexpressibility. Precisely because expression consists of spiritual being rather than ordinary linguistic meanings, revelation represents the epitome of expressibility. This claim anticipates "The Task of the Translator" (1921), which concludes with the observation that sacred scripture is "unconditionally translatable" because "language and revelation are one without any tension."[28] As the communication of its own spiritual being, language expresses itself perfectly, especially the language that by definition expresses spiritual being, namely, revelation. But it is only because revelation does not represent language as a mere sign or means that its expressibility and translatability are possible.

The terms *spiritual being* and *revelation*, however, demand further elaboration, which Benjamin provides by shifting to the spheres of metaphysics and religion. Revelation is specifically identified with religion and not poetry:

> Only the highest spiritual being, as it appears in religion, rests solely on man and on the language in him, whereas all art, not excluding poetry, does not rest on the ultimate essence of language-spirit, but on language-spirit confined to things, even if in consummate beauty.[29]

The contrast between the spiritual being of religion and the beauty of things engenders a contrast between theology and aesthetics. Unlike the soundless language of things, human language has an "immaterial and purely spiritual" community *(Gemeinschaft)* with things; sound symbolizes this community between humans and things.[30] Human language thus differs in kind from the language of things, and the relationship between humans and things becomes symbolic and immaterial. By the same token, human language entails the human relationship to God; Benjamin finds confirmation of this in the Bible: "God breathes his breath into man: this is at once life and mind and language."[31] More to the point: "God's creation is completed when things receive their names from man."[32]

The essay shifts at this point to a reading of Genesis that forms the basis of a quasi-historical theory of language (pre- and post-Lapsarian) as divine revelation, human naming, and, after the Fall, bourgeois language.[33] After the Fall, "in exchange for the immediacy of name damaged by it, a new immediacy arises, the magic of judgment, which no longer rests blissfully in itself."[34] The transition is marked by an uncharacteristic statement of method:

> If in what follows the nature of language is considered on the basis of the first chapter of Genesis, the object is neither biblical interpretation, nor subjection of the Bible to objective consideration as revealed truth, but the discovery of what emerges of itself from the biblical text with regard to the nature of language; and the Bible is only *initially* indispensable for this purpose because the present argument broadly follows it in presupposing language as an ultimate reality, perceptible only in its manifestation, inexplicable and mystical. The Bible, in regarding itself as

a revelation, must necessarily evolve the fundamental linguistic
facts *(die sprachlichen Grundtatsachen).*[35]

What begins as a kind of methodological disclaimer about the
function of the Bible becomes an assertion of its indispensability
to linguistic philosophy. The biblical reflections will not fulfill
conventional expectations as interpretation or as objectively-
considered revealed truth, but rather "what emerges of itself from
the biblical text with regard to the nature of language" *(das, was
aus dem Bibeltext in Ansehung der Natur der Sprache selbst sich
ergibt).*[36] The Bible presupposes *(voraussetzen)* language to be an
ultimate, inexplicable, and mystical reality, and Benjamin adopts
this view. For this reason, and insofar as the Bible considers itself
to be revelation, the Bible forms the basis of the linguistic theory.[37]

The contrast between biblical interpretation and the linguistic
significance of the Bible echoes the distinction between language
as a means and language as the self-expression of spiritual being;
to consider the Bible *objectively* as revealed truth would require
that truth be communicated *through* or by means of biblical language rather than *in* it. Such interpretation, Benjamin suggests,
entails extracting a particular meaning out of the text, whereas his
concern is to identify the spiritual being communicated by the text.
Conventional exegesis would fix the text's meaning, but miss its
spiritual being that is fully expressible only in its original form.
But the contemporary hermeneutical perspective, characterized by
fallen language, has no direct access to the revelation of the Bible.
A complete restructuring of the philosophy of experience and language, outlined in "On the Program of the Coming Philosophy"
(1919), must come first. Still, because the Bible's spiritual being
*(geistige Wesen)* is expressible and because it regards itself as revelation, and because it resides at the "highest spiritual region" of
religion, the Bible epitomizes revelation as a sacred text.

The Bible is only initially *(zunächst)* indispensable to linguistic
philosophy. After it "evolves the fundamental linguistic facts," the
Bible presumably disappears from the center of linguistic philosophy. What begins as an essay on the philosophy of language thus
opens to a philosophy of religion. This is not to say that the Bible
is dispensable; rather, once a linguistic philosophy is grounded in

it, the Bible still underlies ideas and uses of language in the West. The status of the Bible as revelation makes it the foundation for Benjamin's philosophy of language. But the Bible does not transparently communicate the spiritual being of language; it only posits it, initially setting terms for inquiry. Following Genesis, Benjamin identifies language as immediacy, naming, and revelation, all of which contrast post-Lapsarian, bourgeois language.

## The Development of Languages

Benjamin's theory of language can easily be misunderstood as a nostalgic reaffirmation of the categories of revelation, mimesis, purity, and unity.[38] But he never claims to retrieve linguistic purity or to impose an objectivist model of history on the developmental theory of language. Compared to the noninstrumentalized pure language indicated by the Bible, language has deteriorated. The theory of language represents not an historical analysis of language but rather a linguistic model of history.[39]

Language develops in three main stages, according to Benjamin: the pure language of naming associated with Adam's completion of the divine word of creation in Genesis; the deterioration of pure language into multiple, fallen languages in human history; and finally, the persistence of the original pure language in special forms of language, especially sacred texts. For the contemporary philosopher and critic interested in the integrity of language, it becomes necessary to identify the way written language can partially restore or gesture toward pure language. Benjamin appeals to the concepts of revelation and sacred text as the focus for the philosophical and critical retrieval of pure language. Sacred texts represent the highest contemporary expression of pure language and the final stage in linguistic development. The following fragment outlines this progression: "Developmental lineage of language: the separation between the magical and the profane function of language becomes liquidated in favor of the latter. The sacred lies nearer to the profane than the magical."[40] The sacred only appears in contrast to the profane. Sacrality, therefore, is not an ancient category, while magic is. In the development of language, magic precedes sacred and profane forms of language, which are close to one another because each implies the other.[41]

Benjamin's philosophy begins and ends with a theory of language opposing the pure language of naming to the bourgeois language of mere signs. The development of language from the pure name to the mere sign suggests a linguistic theory of history in which individual works and languages literally have lives of their own.[42] Biblical narrative, magic, and theology function initially for Benjamin as critical alternatives to prevailing theories of language. At the same time, the use of biblical and theological history functions as a critique of historicism.[43] Adorno observes:

> He viewed the modern world as archaic not in order to conserve the traces of a purportedly eternal truth but rather to escape the trance-like captivity of bourgeois immanence. He sees his task not in reconstructing the totality of bourgeois society but rather in examining its blinded, nature-bound and diffuse elements under a microscope. . . . Benjamin thus sought to avoid the danger of estrangement and reification, which threaten to transform all observation of capitalism as a system itself into a system.[44]

The theories of language and history are more critical than constructive; they develop alternative forms of inquiry and discourse about language and history.

But why the Bible? How does Benjamin avoid a vicious circle grounding the Bible in his theory and his theory in the Bible? The Bible, through its internal claims and the claims of tradition, regards itself as revelation and therefore "does not know the inexpressible."[45] At the same time, the Bible narrates the origins of language; it both defines and instantiates revelation. This reflexivity sets the stage for a notion of sacred text that combines internalist and externalist features. Benjamin appeals to the Bible as a basis for linguistic philosophy because of its external position of influence in Western culture as well as its internal, reflexive insights into language and sacred texts.

The Bible not only exhibits and defines revelation; it also narrates its loss. The consequences of this loss—the language of the mere sign, the language of judgment, and abstraction—are also associated with the origin of evil.[46] The Bible is an initially indispensable foundation for linguistic philosophy; the pure language of naming constitutes the model and antithesis of ordinary language. But the essay concentrates on describing the difference between pure language and the contemporary language of chatter *(Geschwätz)*[47] without suggesting methods to overcome this difference. The Bible validates pure language and revelation as "fundamental linguistic facts" without making them accessible to language in its currently degraded condition.

Benjamin's essay on language develops a philosophical model out of a biblical-metaphysical conception of language. Language in general, the communication of spiritual being, is distinguished from human language, a reflection of divine language epitomized by naming, but currently degraded as mere sign and means. The essay leaves several issues unresolved, however. Benjamin does not elaborate on the mimetic dimension of human language; if human language is made in God's image, and names ideally express their objects, then this mimesis requires explication. Second, the link between language and text, especially the text of the Bible, needs clarification. Third, the status and function of Benjamin's own writing in relation to sacred texts needs to be clarified. These issues are addressed in what follows and in the next two chapters.

## Archive: "On the Mimetic Faculty" (1933)

An account of the mimetic view of language appears in "Lehre vom Ähnlichen" and its revision, "Über das Mimetisches Vermögen" (both 1933).[48] Although Benjamin composed these brief essays without reference to the language essay (he later asked Scholem to send him a copy for comparison),[49] they fully complement the earlier work. The essays predicate the mimetic faculty as a fundamental human capacity that has decayed progressively through history. In its place goes the category of nonsensuous similarity *(unsinnliche Ähnlichkeit)*, embodied most fully by language in contemporary history.[50] In other words, language symbolizes the lost mimetic capacity. Mimesis appears only indirectly or temporarily through language, for example through handwriting and writing in general:

> Thus writing, along with speech, has become an archive of nonsensuous similarities, nonsensuous correspondences. But this if you will magical[51] side of speech, as of writing, accompanies the other, semiotic side in a not unconnected way. Everything mimetic in speech is rather an established *(fundierte)* intention that can generally only reach something alien, even semiotic, for communicators of speech as their foundation *(Fundus)* in appearance. Thus the literal text of writing *(der Schrift)* is the foundation *(Fundus)*, in which the picture puzzle alone can form itself. ... Writing and speech are that to which clear vision has signed away *(abgetreten)* their [seers' and priests'] old powers in the course of history.[52]

As an archive for the lost mimetic faculty of humanity, language, especially in its written form (and *die Schrift* also denotes Scripture), contains the highest form of the mimetic faculty after its decline in history. The human power of creating similarities has passed into the medium of language, a transfer that, in the essay's second version, has even liquidated magic.[53] Magic, defined in the essay on language as the communicative immediacy of spiritual being in language, has been surpassed by language as the residence of the mimetic faculty.

The "semiotic side" of language (what the essay on language calls "bourgeois" language) conjoins the "magical," mimetic side of language. Thus, even profane reading can mingle with the magical side of language and yield a flash of critical insight:[54] "Rather, everything mimetic in language can, like a flame, manifest itself only through a kind of bearer. This bearer is the semiotic element. Thus the coherence of words or sentences is the bearer through which, like a flash *(blitzartig)*, similarity appears."[55] While Benjamin adheres to a mimetic theory of language, the mimetic function appears only in flashes through human languages, the symbolic archives of the mimetic function. The mimetic faculty deteriorates through history, and language, especially written language, becomes its most important expression, even more important than magic.[56]

As an archive, language is primarily dormant, but it can be reactivated through the proper insight. Post-Lapsarian language becomes a placeholder for pure language and the mimetic faculty. The task of criticism is to reactivate, or at least to consult, this archive. It is noteworthy that Benjamin's letters of this period frequently refer to Scholem's "archive" of Benjamin's writings, which became increasingly important to him as a refugee in the nineteen-thirties.[57] The fact that 1933 was a year of extreme danger for Benjamin did not diminish the urgent tone with which he described his writings on language.[58] Like the political background to the essay on language, the timing of the notes on mimesis suggests he did not consider them to be idle speculations.[59]

## The Song of Moses as a Biblical Archive

If all modern language is an archive of a pure, symbolizing language, then sacred texts are the preeminent archives of pure language. As archives, sacred texts aim for "strict codification" as a "sacred complex."[60] Archives provide permanence and stability; they serve this function whether they are consulted or not. Benjamin's idea of archive came from library collections or even from the collection of his writings kept by Scholem, but the Bible already contains an idea of sacred text as a kind of archive. As we have seen in Deuteronomy 31, YHWH commands Moses to write down and teach the Israelites a Song, recorded in chapter 32, that will act as a lasting witness against them after they become unfaithful. The Song is a multifaceted statement of the covenantal relationship between YHWH and Israel that covers nothing less than the history of Israel from the covenant through transgression and punishment, to the struggles against the nations.

The verbal form of the term for "witness," *'ed*, can mean to repeat, surround, or restore. The related adverbial form, *'od*, notably appearing in 31:2, 27 and 34:10, denotes temporal continuation. The other reference for verbal and nominal forms of the term is "witness." The entry in Brown, Driver, and Briggs suggests that the connotation "witness" comes from *"reiterating,* hence *emphatically affirming."*[61] In other words, repetition over time leads to witness; a characterization that fits perfectly with the Song as a memorized text known to the people and their offspring.

The nominal form of *'ed,* when it means witness or testimony, often has a concrete physical quality, like the stones set up by Jacob and Laban in Gen. 31:41–54, the imitation altar in Joshua 22:28, and the placement of a stone in the divine sanctuary as a witness to the book of the *torah* of God in Joshua 24:22–27; in that text, both the people and the stone are designated witnesses against future transgressions. Probably the most significant use of the term appears in Exodus 31:18 in reference to the "two tablets of *ha'edut,* tablets of stone written with the finger of God." There are also several nominal uses of *'edot* in Deuteronomy (4:45, 6:17, 20), always coupled with *hoq* (literally, something engraved, hence a decree) and *mishpat* (judgment, ordinance), that refer to the *torah* and *mitswot* given by YHWH and Moses to the people. Even within Deuteronomy, then, *'ed* may denote repetition or witness, stone artifact, or written text. The Song, which lives in the mouths and memory of the people and their descendants (31:21) and describes YHWH as a rock forgotten by the people (32:4, 18), resonates with all the semantic valences of *'ed:* repetition, witness, artifact, and covenantal text all describe the Song of Moses. As an archive of the covenant, the Song is by extension an archive of pure language.

## Coda: "Probleme der Sprachsoziologie" (1935)

Despite his developing interests and writing methods during the nineteen-twenties and nineteen-thirties, Benjamin consistently upheld the position of the 1916 essay on language. The encyclopedic review of linguistic literature, which appeared in *Zeitschrift für Sozialforschung,* maintains the same interests in the origins, mimetic function, and autonomy of language that run through the earlier work.[62]

"Problems of the Sociology of Language" covers a vast range of contemporary linguistic, philosophical, psychological, and physiological research, including the work of Saussure, Piaget, Carnap, Husserl, Lévy-Bruhl, and the Grimms. Benjamin organizes this eclectic jumble according to three themes rooted in the tradition of Herder and Humboldt: the origin of language, the link between word and object, and the thought-language relationship. Placing modern research into this intellectual context brings it to the cultural and humanistic level on which Benjamin works best. Without making a sweeping argument, the essay's structure and quotations reflect Benjamin's own position on language quite clearly. He concludes with a long quotation from Kurt Goldstein's study of aphasia that sounds like the 1916 essay on language:

> One could find no better example [than aphasia] to show how false it is to view language as an instrument. . . . As soon as one uses language to produce a living connection to oneself or a person like oneself, language is no longer an instrument, no longer a medium, rather a manifestation, a revelation of our inner being and the physical bond that binds us to our selves and those like ourselves.

"This is the insight," comments Benjamin, "that stands explicitly or implicitly at the beginning of *Sprachsoziologie.*"[63] It is also the insight that motivated much of his own critical practice. (A long passage on Karl Kraus's linguistic theory and practice was omitted from the final version of the essay.)[64] Benjamin's summary of the "linguistic turn" of his time concludes with the insight and the task to which he devoted much of his energy.

Benjamin bases the theory of language as the deteriorated archive of the mimetic faculty on the concept of sacred text, the archive of pure language. The project of restoring pure language poses methodological challenges that Benjamin faced with more self-awareness and resourcefulness than success. But successful restoration of pure language would mean the end of philosophy and society as they are known; Benjamin's main purpose was to show that linguistic theory must seriously consider its historical, conceptual, and metaphysical links to sacred texts.

## NOTES

1. Letter to Ludwig Strauss, 1/7/13, in *GS* 2: 843–44. On Hebbel's nineteenth-century historical drama, see "'El Mayor Monstruo, Los Celos' von Calderon und 'Herodes und Mariamne' von Hebbel," *GS* 2: 246.

2. An earlier version of this essay, "Archive of Pure Language: Language and Sacred Text in Benjamin's Philosophy," appears in *Continuum: The 1994 Annual of Hermeneutics and Social Concern* (1994) 3: 59–80.

3. Benjamin, "On Language as Such and on the Language of Man," in *Reflections*, Peter Demetz, ed., Edmund Jephcott, trans. (New York: Schocken Books, 1986), 322; "Über Sprache überhaupt und über die Sprache des Menschen," *GS*, 2:147.

4. Theodor Adorno, "A Portrait of Walter Benjamin," *Prisms*, trans. Samuel and Shierry Weber (Cambridge, MA: MIT University Press, 1981), 234.

5. Benjamin's distinction between serious and frivolous theological interpretation of Kafka indicates the persistence of his interest in practicing and revising conventional notions of revelation and sacred texts. In a 1934 letter to Scholem on his Kafka essay, Benjamin writes:

> That I do not deny the component of revelation in Kafka's work already follows from my appreciation—by declaring his work to be "distorted"—of its messianic aspect. Kafka's messianic category is the "reversal" or the "studying." You guess correctly that I do not want to shift the path taken by theological interpretation in itself—I practice it myself—but only the arrogant and frivolous *(frechen und leichtfertigen)* form emanating from Prague. *The Correspondence of Walter Benjamin and Gershom Scholem*, 135; *Briefe* 2: 618.

6. One approach that takes composition seriously into account is Jean-Pierre Schobinger's *Variationen zu Walter Benjamins Sprachmeditationen* (Basel/Stuttgart: Schwabe, 1979).

7. Anson Rabinbach shows, through comparison to Benjamin's July 1916 letter to Buber, that this essay "must be read between the lines as an esoteric response to Buber's pro-war and pro-German position"; see "Between Enlightenment and Apocalypse: Benjamin, Bloch and Modern Jewish Messianism," *New German Critique* 34 (Winter, 1985): 105. This controversy is detailed in chapter 4.

8. "On Language," in *Reflections*, 314; "Über Sprache überhaupt und über die Sprache des Menschen," *GS* 2: 140.

9. The essay was written during Benjamin's student days, when he studied Romantic philosophy, including Humboldt's linguistics. See *Briefe*, 400–401.

10. In *Latium und Hellas*, Humboldt writes, "Language is nothing other than the complement of thought, the attempt to elevate external impressions and the still dark inner sensations to clear concepts, and to unite these to the formation of new concepts with each other." Wilhelm von Humboldt, "Über die Natur der Sprache im allgemeinen," in *Schriften zur Sprache*, ed. Michael Bohler (Stuttgart: Philipp Reclam, 1973), 8.

11. Benjamin, *GS* 2:142.

12. Wilhelm von Humboldt, *On Language*, trans. Peter Heath (Cambridge: Cambridge University Press, 1988), 231–32.

13. Ibid., lxiii.

14. "On Language," in *Reflections*, 317; *GS* 2: 142–43. The translation is slightly modified.

15. *GS* 6: 26–27.

16. In "Reflexionen zu Humboldt" (1925), Benjamin writes, "Humboldt naturally overlooks the magical side of language. But he also properly overlooks the mass-psychological and individual psychological (in brief, the anthropological, especially in the pathological sense)" (*GS* 6: 26–27). The notes accompanying this fragment, which were intended for development into a series of lectures on Humboldt, include a page titled "Über den Zusammenhang der Schrift mit der Sprache," *GS* 6: 650.

Benjamin also criticizes as arbitrary Humboldt's view that the word is the most important part of language and comparable to the individual in life (*GS*, 6: 26). He continues, "It is probably of some importance to indicate that Humboldt nowhere in his ideas let a dialectics come to a breakthrough, that he always mediated. There is something stubborn in Humboldt's style and progress of thought," *GS*, 6: 27.

17. "On Language," in *Reflections*, 317.

18. This begins the second part of the essay, which concerns human language in particular. The two parts of the essay correspond not only to language in general and human language in particular but also to the philosophical and the theological (biblical), and to the synchronic and the diachronic.

19. Ibid., 318.

20. "On Language," in *Reflections*, 317.

21. Ibid., 318.

22. Ibid., 324, 330.

23. "On Language," 318. The translation of *geistig* here as "mental" is misleading; "spiritual," in the strict sense of relation to spirit as *Geist*, is more accurate, *GS* 2: 142.

24. "Der Mensch ist der Nennende, daran erkennen wir, dass aus ihm die reine Sprache spricht," *GS* 2: 144.

25. See "On Language," in *Reflections*, 327–28, and "Critique of Violence," in *Reflections*, 277–300.

26. Jewish tradition frequently refers to God as *hashem*, "the Name." See Benjamin's fragment, "Über Das Rätsel und Das Geheimnis," in which Benjamin contrasts mythical, fairy-tale naming as riddle (*Rätsel*) with biblical naming as secret or mystery *(Geheimnis):* "Der jüdische Name (der hebräische) ist ein Geheimnis," *GS* 6: 17–18.

27. "On Language," in *Reflections*, 321; "Über Sprache," in *GS* 2: 146.

28. "The Task of the Translator," in *Illuminations*, 82.

29. "On Language," in *Reflections*, 321.

30. "Über Sprache," in *GS* 2: 147.

31. "On Language," in *Reflections*, 319.

32. Ibid.

33. The analysis of Benjamin's Genesis interpretation appears in chapter 5.

34. Ibid., 328.

35. Ibid., 322; "Über Sprache," in *GS* 2: 147.

36. "Über Sprache," in *GS* 2: 147.

37. "Basis" in this sense does not mean origin in any historical sense, as Stéphane Mosès points out in "L'idée d'origine chez Walter Benjamin," in *Walter Benjamin et Paris*, ed. Heinz Wismann (Paris: Editions du Cerf, 1986), 811.

38. See Jürgen Habermas, "Consciousness-Raising or Redemptive Criticism—The Contemporaneity of Walter Benjamin," trans. Philip Brewster and Carl Howard Buchner, *New German Critique* 17 (1979): 30–59.

39. See, for example, the notion of history in "The Task of the Translator" (in *Illuminations*): "The idea of life and afterlife in works of art should be regarded with an entirely unmetaphorical objectivity.... The concept of life is given its due only if everything that has a history of its own, and is not merely the setting for history, is credited with life," (71).

40. *GS*, 2: 956.

41. Magic precedes religion (and hence the sacred) in "The Work of Art in the Age of Its Technical Reproducibility" *(Illuminations*, 223). See also the passage on sacred and profane texts in "One-Way Street," in *Reflections*, 68.

42. "The Task of the Translator," in *Illuminations*, 71.

43. See "Theses on the Philosophy of History," in *Illuminations*, 253–64.

44. Adorno, "A Portrait of Walter Benjamin," in *Prisms*, 236.

45. Ibid., 321. Deuteronomy 31–34 is an example of a biblical text with internal claims to sacred status (see chapter 1); Genesis, on the other hand, depends more on the claims of tradition.

46. *The Origin of German Tragic Drama*, 233.

47. "Über Sprache," in *GS* 2: 153.

48. *GS* 2: 204–10 and 210–13, respectively.

49. Letter to Scholem, May 23, 1933, *Briefe* 2: 575.

50. "Über das Mimetische Vermögen," *GS* 2: 211–12.

51. The term *magische* is removed from the later version.

52. "Lehre vom Ähnlichen," *GS* 2: 208–9.

53. "Über das Mimetisches Vermögen," *GS* 2: 213.

54. "Lehre vom Ähnlichen," *GS* 2: 209–10.

55. "On the Mimetic Faculty," in *Reflections*, 334.

56. Ibid., 335–36.

57. See the 1933 letters to Scholem, *Briefe* 2: 562, 565, 567.

58. Ibid., 566.

59. See the Appendix, which describes Benjamin's preoccupation with bringing a heavy case full of papers on his attempt to escape from Vichy France in 1940.

60. *The Origin of German Tragic Drama*, 175.

61. Francis Brown, S. R. Driver, and C. A. Briggs, *A Hebrew and English Lexicon of the Old Testament* (Oxford: Oxford University Press, 1951), 729.

62. *GS* 3: 452–80.

63. *GS* 3: 480.

64. *GS* 3: 675.

# CHAPTER 3

# The Task:
# "To Regain Pure Language"

And so the real world could well constitute a task, in the sense that it would be a question of penetrating so deeply into everything real as to reveal thereby an objective interpretation of the world. In the light of such a task of penetration it is not surprising that the philosopher of the *Monadology* was also the founder of infinitesimal calculus. The idea is a monad—that means briefly: every idea contains the image of the world.[1]

## History and Praxis:
## "The Task of the Translator" (1921)

*B*enjamin's essay on language identifies translation as part of the development toward the unity of divine language, an idea he elaborated five years later in "The Task of the Translator."[2] In the preface to his translation of Baudelaire's *Tableaux Parisiens,* Benjamin argues that the purpose of great literature and Scripture is not to communicate meaning but rather to demonstrate a mode of expression. Repeating a question from the essay on language, "What does language communicate?" *(Was teilt die Sprache mit?),* Benjamin presents translation both as a topic within linguistic theory and as a partial solution to its decline. Translation reveals the essential kinship of languages in their *intention,* or intended reference (as opposed to their particular structure and meaning).[3]

All languages are linked by their intentions, but they differ in their modes of intention: "The words *Brot* and *pain* 'intend' the same object, but the modes of this intention are not the same."[4] According to Benjamin, the two words mean the same thing, but they do so in different modes. The mode of any given language is somehow incomplete in itself:

> In the individual, unsupplemented languages, meaning is never found in relative independence, as in individual words or sentences; rather it is in a constant state of flux *(Wandel)*—until it is able to emerge as pure language from the harmony of all the various modes of intention. Until then, it remains hidden in the languages. If, however, these languages continue to grow in this manner until the messianic end of their history, it is translation which catches fire on the eternal afterlife of the works and the perpetual renewal *(Aufleben)* of languages. Translation keeps putting the sacred growth of languages to the test: How far removed is their hidden meaning from revelation, how close can it be brought by the knowledge of this remoteness?[5]

Translation functions for works and for individual languages as an index of how closely they approach pure language and revelation. Languages have a sacred growth and a messianic end; this is to say that the inner structure and purpose of languages is incomplete without the recovery of pure language; hence the unstable flux of meaning in languages.[6] It is not to say, however, that the history of languages is determined in any clear way. The "messianic end" of languages functions rather as the theoretical limit, goal, and antipode to historical languages.[7] Accordingly, the translation of sacred texts plays a central role:

> Where a text is identical with truth or dogma, where it is supposed to be "the true language" in all its literalness and without the mediation of meaning, this text is unconditionally translatable.... All great texts contain their potential translation between the lines; this is true to the highest degree of sacred writings. The interlinear version of the Scriptures is the prototype or ideal of all translation.[8]

For Benjamin, translation is a gesture toward the mystical reunion of all languages, and Scripture, which by definition implies this unity, is the most translatable of all texts. This does not mean that translating Scripture is literally easier than other texts; rather, the universality of Scripture places it atop a hierarchy of literature: what could be more universal than The Word?

The purpose of literary and sacred works is to affirm human existence, not to please an audience or spectator.[9] Accordingly, works are not intended to communicate information but rather posit "the existence and nature of man": "No poem is intended for the reader, no picture for the beholder, no symphony for the listener."[10] It follows from this that translations of literature and Scripture are not intended to communicate mere information. For, he argues, "If the original does not exist for the reader's sake, how could the translation be understood on the basis of this premise?"[11]

Just as works of art posit life, they also have a life and afterlife *(Fortleben)* of their own. Translations of literature and Scripture arise only in this stage of afterlife.[12] In other words, the work has already undergone a transformation by the time it gains the acclaim and renown that call for translations. This continued life marks a positive development for the work; as it gets older, it reaches a higher degree of "fame" and "abundant flowering."[13] Translation is a hallmark, then, of great literary works. It connects the different languages together for the purpose of sharing the afterlife, not the mere meaning, of literary and sacred works. Benjamin generalizes the connective role of translation in the principle that all languages are related in a concept of "pure language":

> Translation thus ultimately serves the purpose of expressing the central reciprocal relationship between languages. It cannot possibly reveal *(offenbaren)* or establish *(herstellen)* this hidden relationship itself; but it can represent *(darstellen)* it by realizing it in embryonic or intensive form. . . . All suprahistorical kinship of languages rests in the intention underlying each language as a whole—an intention, however, which no single language can attain by itself but which is realized only by the totality of their intentions supplementing each other: pure language.[14]

The translator cannot reveal or establish the relationship among languages but can represent this relationship and realize *(verwirklichten)* it in embryonic form. Here Benjamin addresses the question of his own linguistic *praxis.* Translating a text, like doing philosophy,[15] is clearly distinguished from and yet attached to revelation.

Here, as in the essays on language and mimesis, philosophy of language connects with philosophy of religion: "An instant and final rather than a temporary and provisional solution of this foreignness [of languages] remains out of the reach of mankind; at any rate, it eludes any direct attempt. Indirectly, however, the growth of religions ripens the hidden seed into a higher development of language."[16] The growth of religions parallels the growth of (pure) language, but not as a result of any deliberate human action, not even translation. Benjamin never elaborates on this growth of religions, but as the essay progresses he strengthens the claim to the restorative function of translation: "To relieve [pure language] of this [alien meaning], to turn the symbolizing into the symbolized, to regain *(zurückzugewinnen)* pure language fully formed in the linguistic flux, is the tremendous and only capacity of translation."[17] The essay applies a practical method of translation to the recovery of pure language: "It is the task of the translator to release in his own language that pure language which is under the spell of another, to liberate the language imprisoned in a work in his re-creation of that work."[18] The work of translation is not only to represent *(darstellen)* pure language but also to regain it. The analogy between translation and the growth of religions becomes substantial at this point, since both terms play a constructive role in the aspiration to recover pure language; both are described in terms of ripening the seed of language.[19] The analogy between religion and translation, though never explicitly elaborated in the essay, culminates in the final paragraph where sacred texts are defined as being unconditionally translatable.

Benjamin contends that "translatability is an essential quality of certain works, which is not to say that it is essential that they be translated; it means rather that a specific significance inherent in the original manifests itself in its translatability."[20] In other words, translatability corresponds to the scriptural function of a text. Since sacred texts are by definition immediately expressible truth, they are "unconditionally translatable." This claim parallels that of the language essay, where "revelation" is the fully expressed language of naming.

But what is this "pure language" and what does Benjamin mean when he says that translation expresses the "kinship of languages"? Two interpretations are possible. First, Benjamin indicates that translations draw attention to the relationships among languages. Since language is the vehicle for the life or intention posited by literary works, languages may achieve this task in similar ways. A second, deeper meaning of "pure language" and translation follows from this. Translation discloses pure language, thus the practice of translating moves history closer to a time of the reunification of languages. And yet, this reunion is impossible: "the problem of ripening the seed of pure language in a translation seems to be insoluble."[21] Translation becomes a gesture—"midway between poetry and doctrine"—toward an unattainable Utopia of perfect linguistic unity and harmony between word and truth.[22]

It is significant that Benjamin writes this in a preface to his own translation of Baudelaire's poetry. The reflections on translation seem to come directly from experience. Benjamin's own work as a translator constitutes a praxis that participates, however indirectly, in the recovery of pure language. Translation is a dialectical process containing two parallel progressions. On the one hand, certain texts, especially sacred texts, invite translation; in fact, their capacity to disclose truth demands translation. Literary and sacred texts go through the progressive stages of life and afterlife, always gaining in value, and translations crown works at the peak of their fruition. At the same time, translation participates in the ascent to pure language. The inherent merit of the work and the constructive activity of translating create a double-gain. The newly-created language of translations lies in the fissures between the two languages involved: "A real translation is transparent; it does not cover the original, does not block its light, but allows the pure language, as though reinforced by its own medium, to shine upon the original all the more fully."[23] The praxis of translating achieves more than just the transfer of works from one tongue to another; it reveals what the two languages have in common, and also the essence of the work apart from the technical exigencies of either language.

In the translation of sacred texts, the disclosure of truth is dual. On the one hand, the text's mode of expression (not meaning) is already identical with truth, so any faithful translation must de facto convey that truth; in addition, translation contributes to the restoration of pure language. But the historical process of linguistic decline and restoration is complex and uncertain, since each language and even each great work has a life and afterlife of its own. Translation, even the translation of sacred texts, is no guarantee of the full restoration of pure language.

## *Philosophy as Restorative Praxis*

The task of the philosopher parallels the task of the translator. In the prologue to the 1925 *Trauerspiel* study, Benjamin draws a sharp distinction between philosophy and revelation:

> It is the task of the philosopher to restore *(wieder einzusetzen)*, by representation *(Darstellung)*, the primacy of the symbolic character of the word, in which the idea is given self-consciousness, and that is the opposite of all outwardly-directed communication. Since philosophy may not presume to speak in the tones of revelation, this can only be achieved by recalling in memory the primordial form of perception.[24]

It is not Plato but Adam who is the "father of mankind as well as the father of philosophy."[25] Benjamin's analysis of the task of philosophy in the *Trauerspiel* study follows the model of Adamic naming developed in the essay on language. Philosophy represents the primarily symbolic character of the word through memory; in the study of allegorical baroque drama, philosophy identifies and expresses the unique idea of the *Trauerspiel.* This highly conventional and melancholy form of allegory is situated between a sacred tradition it seeks to recover and a profane present it tries to transform.

A constitutive factor of baroque drama was the "contemplative necessities which are implicit in the contemporary theological situation. One of these, consequent upon the total disappearance of eschatology, is the attempt to find, in a reversion to a bare state of creation, consolation for the renunciation of a state of grace."[26] The *Trauerspiel* study seeks more than insight into an almost-forgotten literary genre; it continues the project, set out in the essay on language, of pursuing the pure language posited by the Bible. Because of its particular sensitivity to the fallen state of language, the seventeenth-century German baroque drama captures Benjamin's attention in his philosophical search to restore pure language. Any such recovery, however, must always be retrospective and abstract, seen through the eyes of previous allegorical attempts to understand it: "The allegorical has its existence in abstractions; as an abstraction, as a faculty of the spirit of language itself, it is at home in the Fall."[27] In Benjamin's linguistic universe, philosophy and allegory both pursue the lost pure language of naming through the fallen language of judgment and abstraction.

The broad purpose of philosophy is outlined by Benjamin in "Über das Programm der kommenden Philosophie" (1917–18), the programmatic essay that takes Kant's epistemology as a starting-point for the redirection of philosophy.[28] Attacking Kant's concept of experience *(Erfahrung)* as an uncritically mythological metaphysics,[29] Benjamin suggests a revision of Kant's notions of knowledge and experience with respect to language:

> The great restructuration and correction which must be performed upon the concept of experience ... can only be attained by relating knowledge to language, such as was attempted by Hamann during Kant's lifetime. For Kant, the consciousness that philosophical knowledge was absolutely certain and *a priori,* the consciousness of that aspect of philosophy in which it is fully the peer of mathematics, caused the fact that all philosophical knowledge has its unique expression in language and not in formulae or numbers to go almost completely untreated. ... *A concept of knowledge gained from reflection on the linguistic nature of knowledge will create a corresponding concept of experience which will also encompass regions that Kant failed to integrate into his system. The realm of religion should be mentioned as the foremost of these.* And thus the demand upon the philosophy of the future can finally be put in these words: to create on the basis of the Kantian system a

concept of knowledge to which a concept of experience corresponds, of which the knowledge is the doctrine. Such a philosophy in its universal element would either itself be designated as theology or would be super-ordinated to theology to the extent that it contains historically philosophical elements.[30]

Benjamin juxtaposes two failings in Kant's notion of experience: inattention to language and inattention to religion. By acknowledging the linguistic character of knowledge, Benjamin's revised concept of experience incorporates religious experience. The result would be a conflation of philosophy with religion and theology. Whereas philosophy alone is unable to discover the unity of existence, religion constitutes the concrete totality of experience.[31] Of course, the program sketched here was never realized by Benjamin, and its ambitious character suggests that such was not his intention; the course charted for philosophy represents a testing of philosophical boundaries consistent with the broader philosophical task of restoring pure language.[32]

## Sacred Texts and the
### Trauerspiel *Study (1925)*

If language is the archive of the mimetic function and a deteriorated version of the pure language of naming, then the question becomes: What forms of language give us the most insight into pure language? One answer to this question is, of course, Benjamin's own critical writings. In fact, Benjamin's disparate works can be understood as a series of compositional experiments designed to illuminate the problems of language and knowledge he identified in his earliest work.[33] But the major source of insight into pure language comes from sacred texts. Why Benjamin thinks this is so and what he means by sacred text are difficult questions to answer, partly because he addresses them in unconventional and sketchy ways. The most sustained discussion of sacred texts appears in the second part of the 1923 study of German baroque drama, "Allegory and Trauerspiel":

All of the [profane] things which are used to signify derive, from the very fact of their pointing to something else, a power

which makes them appear no longer commensurable with profane things, which raises them onto a higher plane, and which
can, indeed, sanctify them. Considered in allegorical terms,
then, the profane world is both elevated and devalued *(erhoben
wie entwertet)*. . . . The sanctity of what is written is inextricably
bound up with the idea of its strict codification. For sacred
script always takes the form of certain complexes [or systems:
*Komplex*] of words which ultimately constitute, or aspire to
become, one single and inalterable complex.[34]

On the level of content, allegory exhibits a dialectic of the sacred
and the profane. The effort to elevate the profane world to the
sacred also devalues it, because any one element can represent any
other. On the other hand, this interpretive fluidity has the opposite
effect of sanctifying the profane signifier.[35] On the level of form,
allegory exhibits a dialectic of convention and expression. Both
elements appear in all allegory and sacred texts, even in the
convention-heavy German baroque drama, which he describes as
"expression of convention."

The dialectical nature of allegory applies to writing itself. Unlike
speech, writing tends toward codification (or convention) in order
to acquire sacred authority. Sacred texts thus take the form of
systems and hieroglyphics. Here the notion of writing as an archive
of the mimetic faculty and the pure language of naming finds expression in the fascination with picture languages, visual images, and
heraldry characteristic of baroque allegory. This is not to say that
sacred texts ever actually attain absolute codification; on the contrary, there is "always a conflict between sacred standing and profane comprehensibility." Writing stands apart from speech in that
its dignity *(Würde)* and sacrality depend on its codification; speech,
unlike writing, can be lively and dignified at the same time. The
codification of sacred texts relates to their capacity to represent
pure language: the codified system tends to communicate its own
linguistic and spiritual being rather than convey ordinary meaning
as a mere sign.

This view explains the particular "bombast" *(Schwulst)* of the
German *Trauerspiel:* "For its writing does not achieve transcendence by being voiced; rather does the world of written language

remain self-sufficient and intent on the display of its own substance. Written language and sound confront each other in tense polarity."[36] Like the notion of writing as an archive of the deteriorated mimetic faculty, or the notion of sacred texts as unconditionally translatable revelation, the *Trauerspiel* views writing in general and sacred texts in particular as the best and most valid modes of expression from the standpoint of philosophy. Benjamin celebrates the bombastic style of the *Trauerspiel* because he sees it as an authentic attempt at linguistic self-expression. The task of philosophy is to restore the pure language of naming from the standpoint of the Fall. Rejecting the romantic nostalgia for the purity and primacy of speech,[37] Benjamin chooses the more indirect path of representing pure language as it appears in texts.

Sacred texts arise out of the fallen language of a profane world. Though capable of revelation, sacred texts constitute a belated gesture toward recovering the spoken pure language of naming out of the written language of the mere sign. The paradigmatic sacred text, the Bible, communicates its own spiritual being insofar as it refuses to communicate meaning in the ordinary way. But in order to be accessible at all, the sacred text must strike a compromise between revelation and ordinary language. Such a compromise is essential to writing and becomes the model for all writing. Only writing—especially the writing of sacred texts—makes possible the recovery of pure language for contemporary understanding: "The Bible must evolve the fundamental linguistic facts."

What interests Benjamin in baroque allegory is the melancholy gravity with which it expresses the contradictions inherent in writing: "Allegory established itself most permanently where transitoriness and eternity confronted each other most closely."[38] Without the reassuring comfort of eschatology, the *Trauerspiel* sought, "in a reversion to a bare state of creation, consolation for the renunciation of a state of grace."[39] Baroque allegory correlates biblical revelation with its own fallen hermeneutical perspective; sacred and profane texts are intertwining features of the contemporary linguistic landscape. The study of allegory delineates the attempt to restore pure language in a fallen linguistic world. Like allegory, later cultural forms such as Baudelaire's poetry and surrealist literature represent successive instances of the loss of pure language. Many of the later works—*Einbahnstrasse,* the studies of Baudelaire in the *Passagen-Werk,* and the essay on the concept of history—bear this out.

### The Text of Modern Culture: One-Way Street (1926)

*One-Way Street* marks a new direction in Benjamin's philosophy, with its novel compositions about the phenomena of modern urban culture; the influences of psychoanalysis, Marxism, and surrealism are also evident here.[40] Like allegory, modern life presents experience with contradictions. The abiding interest of this collection of pithy theses, aphorisms, anecdotes, and dreams is how to make the praxis of writing relevant and valuable to modern experience. Most of the passages are entitled with a phrase from everyday life, such as "Post No Bills" and "Germans, Drink German Beer!" Like the Dadaists and their found objects, Benjamin creatively manipulates these banal headings to relate in surprising ways to unrelated contexts. *One-Way Street* constitutes a playful language experiment that explores the simultaneously progressive and regressive, sacred and profane manifestations of modern culture.

*One-Way Street* dates from the period often associated with Benjamin's turn to Marxism.[41] This characterization overlooks, however, the presence of materialist elements in Benjamin's earlier work; the unorthodox nature of Benjamin's Marxism;[42] and the text's reliance on metaphors of religion, writing, and the Bible. Consider the blend of Marxist and religious vocabulary in the entry titled "Marseille Cathedral":

> On the facade are the waiting rooms, recognizable by the interiors, where the first to fourth traveling classes (though before God they are all equal) are squeezed as if between trunks in their spiritual belongings; they sit and read in hymnals that look, with their concordances and cross-references, like international railway guides. . . . This is the religious train station of Marseille.[43]

*Einbahnstrasse* also explores the dynamics of writing in two numbered sets of principles; the first is a satire on scholarly writing called "Teaching Aid: Principles of the Weighty Tome, or How to Write Fat Books," and the second, more serious list is "Post No Bills: The Writer's Technique in Thirteen Theses."[44] The satire on academic writing probably originates in Benjamin's own experience of the rejection of his *Habilitationsschrift* (the *Trauerspiel* study) by the University of Frankfurt;[45] for example: "Conceptual distinctions laboriously arrived at in the text are to be obliterated again in the relevant notes."[46] The theses on the writer's technique also have an autobiographical flavor: "Let no thought pass incognito, and keep your notebook as strictly as the authorities keep their register of aliens."[47] Benjamin's notion of language as self-communication informs the following principle: "Keep your pen aloof from inspiration *(Eingebung)*, which it will then attract with magnetic power. The more circumspectly you delay writing down an idea, the more maturely developed it will be on surrendering itself. Speech conquers thought, but writing commands it *(Die Rede erobert den Gedanken, aber die Schrift beherrscht ihn).* "[48]

Sacred texts, like all great works, are always retrospective; they attain their full significance only in their afterlife *(Fortleben)*, through translation, for example;[49] like the baroque allegory, there is something belated about sacred texts in general. The distinction between sacred and profane texts is relatively recent and dialectical; it reflects the contradictions inherent in language after the Fall: "The undialectic neo-Kantian mode of thought is not able to grasp the synthesis which is reached in allegorical writing as a result of the conflict between theological and artistic intentions, a synthesis not so much in the sense of a peace as a *treuga dei* between the conflicting opinions."[50] Writing is privileged over speech as an archive of pure language because it is conducive to interpretive fluidity and the representation of pure language. Texts allow for the careful philosophical and critical reflection of the modern thinker; sacred texts, with the Bible as the primary case, represent the inherent contradictions of language and the traces of the lost pure language of naming.

## Walter Benjamin's Dialectical Compositions

The view of sacred text as linguistic restoration through philosophy poses a challenge to Benjamin's own writing. Because his objective is to restore language that is normative but not directly accessible to contemporary understanding, methods of composition are essential to his philosophical praxis. In other words, a theory of language that promotes the self-communication of language over the communication of meaning must find modes of expression that are convincing without reinforcing the rationalistic, instrumentalizing tendencies of conventional philosophy.[51] I suggest that the changes in Benjamin's work reflect revisions in compositional strategy and different subject matter (e.g., baroque allegory, surrealism, Kafka) rather than modifications of his basic project. Benjamin utilized at least four compositional strategies to accommodate his theory of language: the rhetoric of the task, the experimental mixing of genres, aphoristic fragments, and quotation.

## The Rhetoric of the Task

While considering dissertation topics in 1918, Benjamin became interested in the Kantian notion that science *(Wissenschaft)* is an endless task.[52] As a compositional strategy, the rhetoric of the task goes beyond saying that science or philosophy is always incomplete. For Benjamin, the point becomes an opportunity to merge the terms and discourses of various fields under the heading of a single project. His most Kantian work, "On the Program of the Coming Philosophy," proposes to blend religion and philosophy in the pursuit of a new understanding of experience.[53] The essay emphasizes the task of philosophy rather than the steps toward its attainment.[54]

The clearest example of the rhetoric of the task appears in "The Task of the Translator," where descriptions of the task of translation, as opposed to the assertions of its accomplishment, drive the essay. The ultimate goal of recovering pure language seems unattainable: "If the task of the translator is viewed in this light, the roads toward a solution seem to be all the more obscure and impenetrable."[55] Nevertheless, the task continues to have normative force, and its goal appears to be accomplished by degrees. In an even more radical fashion, "Toward the Critique of Violence" (1921) proposes a number of mutually conflicting alternatives (e.g., the proletarian general strike vs. the conference) to the bourgeois system of law emerging from the natural law tradition. All three of these essays articulate the steps required to alleviate a philosophical problem without claiming to achieve a solution. In every case, the task is associated with rethinking the problem in linguistic and religious terms.[56] The rhetoric of the task allows a critical perspective on philosophical problems and makes space for the paradox of recovering the unrecoverable pure language of naming.[57] Because of the epistemological and linguistic consequences of the Fall, the critical understanding of sacred texts offers special insight into this paradox.

With the task at hand unfinished, Benjamin often concludes his essays with a gesture to supernatural or occult phenomena. These maneuvers refocus discussion from the expressible to the inexpressible, from the value of discursive knowledge to its limitations. Most of all, these dramatic conclusions attempt, however partially, to recover pure language. The essay on translation, for instance, concludes with the assertion that the interlinear version of the Bible is the ideal of all translation.[58]

Angels are Benjamin's favorite supernatural figures. "Karl Kraus" is compared to a Talmudic angel that lives just long enough to raise its voice to God;[59] the image anticipates the "Angelus Novus" of "On the Concept of History" and the closing of "The Storyteller": "The storyteller—that is the man who allows the wick of his life to be completely consumed by the gentle flame of his storytelling."[60] Anachronistic and ephemeral, angels and storytellers represent a "praxis" that is "no longer current."[61] They are equally messianic and apocalyptic: "The angel would like to stay, awaken the dead, and make whole what has been smashed. But a storm is blowing from Paradise; it has got caught in his wings with such violence that the angel can no longer close them."[62]

The occult practices of soothsaying, astrology, graphology, and physiognomy appear in the conclusions of "On the Mimetic Faculty," "Fate and Character," and "On the Concept of History."[63] Benjamin's interest in the occult is neither superstitious nor dismissive; he proposes a dialectical approach that takes the phenomena seriously without endorsing them.[64] Like allegory and the essays themselves, "occult praxis" recognizes pure language but fails to recover it.

## Genre Combination

Benjamin combines many genres in the essays on language, translation, storytelling, violence, and in the *Trauerspiel* study and *One-Way Street*. These texts describe the deterioration and recovery of language through various combinations: for example, biblical interpretation and philosophy in the essay on language; philosophy and literary criticism in the *Trauerspiel* study; the experimental juxtapositions of dreams, aphorisms, and anecdotes in *Einbahnstrasse;* and philosophy and theology in "Program." "Toward the Critique of Violence" combines natural law philosophy, the French syndicalist Georges Sorel's idea of the general strike, the idea of negotiated conflict resolution, and a theological meditation on Numbers 16.[65] Instead of raising and discussing only one of these issues, Benjamin sets them side by side almost as a challenge, as if to say that any full account of violence must consider all sides of the issue. Like a montage, the combination of genres stimulates critical consciousness by complicating and disrupting ordinary discourse.

Such mixing of genres to express complexity of meaning is not unusual in the Bible. In Deuteronomy, the Song of Moses (chapter 32) is a poem of vast scope about the relationship between YHWH and Israel. In terms of genre, the poem has didactic, lyrical, and narrative components. In biblical terms, we may ask whether to view it more properly as a *shirah* (song), as the text indicates, or as a *maskil* (didactic poem), the term applied to its close parallel, Psalm 78.[66] The Song also contains a lawsuit *(rîb)* against Israel; it calls the cosmos and nations as witnesses. It may also be described as a character portrait of YHWH or as a meditation on divine justice in history. Through its combination of genres, the poem represents a multifaceted statement of the covenantal relationship between YHWH and Israel.

## Quotation

In the Arcades project, which examines the objectworld of nineteenth-century Paris, the technique of quotation serves, like translation, to attend to pure language by disrupting the flow of modern language. Pages and pages of quotations without commentary fill the manuscripts of the *Passagen-Werk*. Benjamin describes this method as "literary montage": "I have nothing to say. Only to show."[67] Benjamin developed the idea in his 1931 essay on Karl Kraus, the Austrian satirical journalist whom he admired: "In the quotation that both saves and chastises, language proves the matrix of justice. It summons the word by its name, wrenches it destructively from its context, but precisely thereby calls it back to its origin."[68]

With quotation, the rhetoric of the task, and combined genres, the praxis of writing takes on philosophical, theological, and political dimensions as the way to recover pure language. Though often only implicitly, the Bible provides a model for Benjamin's writing as the paradigmatic archive of pure language.

### NOTES

1. *The Origin of German Tragic Drama*, 48.
2. "Über Sprache," *GS* 2: 157.
3. "The Task of the Translator," in *Illuminations*, 73–74; *GS* 4: 9–21.
4. Ibid.
5. Ibid., with some modifications based on the original, *GS* 4: 14.
6. Derrida notes that "This is the most Babelian note in an analysis of sacred writing as the model and the limit of all writing." Jacques Derrida, "Des Tours de Babel," trans. Joseph F. Graham, in *Difference in Translation*, Joseph F. Graham, ed. (Ithaca: Cornell University Press, 1985), 191.
7. See "Theologico-Political Fragment," in *Reflections*, 312–13, and "On Language," in *Reflections*.
8. "The Task of the Translator," in *Illuminations*, 82.
9. Ibid., 69.
10. Ibid.
11. Ibid., 70. One practical consequence of this view for Benjamin's theory of translation is an emphasis on a literal method of translation. This follows from the belief that the life or intention of a great work is more important than its meaning (ibid., 72, 76).
12. Ibid., 71. See also the notion of a progressive separation between a work's subject matter *(Sachgehalt)*, the provenance of commentary, and truth content *(Wahrheitsgehalt)*, the object of criticism, in the essay on Goethe's *Elective Affinities*, *GS* 1: 125–26 and "Central Park," trans. Lloyd Spencer, in *New German Critique* 34 (1985): 54, 58 n.43.

13. "The Task of the Translator," in *Illuminations*, 71–72.

14. Ibid.; "Die Aufgabe des Übersetzers," 12.

15. See *The Origin of German Tragic Drama*, 36–37.

16. "The Task of the Translator," in *Illuminations*, 75.

17. Ibid., 80; "Die Aufgabe," 19.

18. Ibid.

19. Ibid., 75, 77.

20. Ibid., 71.

21. Ibid., 77.

22. Ibid.

23. Ibid., 79.

24. *The Origin of German Tragic Drama*, 36–37; GS 1: 216–17.

25. Ibid., 37.

26. Ibid., 80–81.

27. Ibid., 234.

28. GS 2: 157–71, and "On the Program of the Coming Philosophy," trans. Mark Ritter, in *Benjamin: Philosophy, Aesthetics, History*, ed. Gary Smith (Chicago: University of Chicago Press, 1989), 1–12.

29. "Die Kantische 'Erfahrung' ist in *dieser* Hinsicht, was die naive Vorstellung vom Empfangen der Wahrnegmungen angeht, Metaphysik oder Mythologie und zwar nur eine moderne und religiös besonders unfruchtbare," GS 2: 162.

30. "On the Program of the Coming Philosophy," 9–10, emphasis added.

31. Ibid., 11.

32. See the 1912 "Dialog über die Religiosität der Gegenwart," which traces a modern crisis and revision of religion to Kant, GS 2: 16–35. See also "Erfahrung und Armut," GS 2: 213.

33. See the section on Benjamin's compositions at the conclusion to this chapter.

34. *The Origin of German Tragic Drama*, 175; GS 1: 351.

35. The dialectical interrelationship between sacred and profane, which characterizes Benjamin's notion of sacred text as an archive of pure language, has a parallel in the opposition between war and peace: "Indeed, the word 'peace,' in the sense in which it is the correlative to the word 'war' ... denotes this *a priori*, necessary sanctioning [of military violence], regardless of all other legal conditions, of every victory," "The Critique of Violence," 283.

36. *The Origin of German Tragic Drama*, 201; GS 1: 376.

37. See, for example, *The Origin of German Tragic Drama*, 201–5 and "Surrealism," in *Reflections*, 189.

38. *The Origin of German Tragic Drama*, 224.

39. Ibid., 80–81.

40. Excerpted in *Reflections*, 61–94.

41. See, for example, Gershom Sholem, *Walter Benjamin: The Story of a Friendship*, trans. Harry Zohn (New York: Schocken, 1981), 122–24. The book is inscribed to Asja Lacis, the Latvian revolutionary whom Benjamin followed to Moscow in 1926. See *Moskauer Tagebuch*, GS 6: 292–409.

42. See letter to Scholem, 5/6/34, *Briefe* 2:603–6; see also Leandro Konder, "Benjamin und die Revolution," in *Für Walter Benjamin*, ed. Ingrid and Konrad Scheurmann (Frankfurt: Suhrkamp, 1002), 226–32.

43. *GS* 4: 124.

44. "One-Way Street," in *Reflections*, 81. There are also "Thirteen Theses against Snobs," "The Technique of Critics in Thirteen Theses," and thirteen untitled aphorisms that each begin with the phrase "Books and Prostitutes," *Einbahnstrasse*, 49–54.

45. See Irving Wohlfarth, "Resentment Begins at Home: Nietzsche, Benjamin, and the University," in *On Walter Benjamin*, ed. Gary Smith (Cambridge, MA: MIT Press, 1988), 224–59.

46. "One-Way Street," 79.

47. Ibid., 81.

48. Ibid., 81; *Einbahnstrasse*, 47–48.

49. "The translation, ironically, transplants the original into a more definitive linguistic realm since it can no longer be displaced by a secondary rendering," ("The Task of the Translator," in *Illuminations*, 75).

50. *The Origin of German Tragic Drama*, 177.

51. This position is already anticipated in the *Trauerspiel* study, for example in the criticism of rationalism and idealism on linguistic grounds in the prologue. See also the attack on the neo-Kantian conception of allegory, *The Origin of German Tragic Drama*, 177.

52. Letter to Scholem, July 23, 1917, *Briefe* 1: 161, see McCole, p. 80. The phrase also appears more casually in another letter to Scholem the following year (March 30, 1918), *Briefe* 1: 180.

53. The essay begins, in fact, with a statement of the "central task of the coming philosophy," *GS* 2: 157–71.

54. "Yet here, where we are concerned only with a program of research and not with proof, only this much need be said: no matter how necessary and inevitable it may be to reconstruct, on the basis of a new transcendental logic, the realm of dialectics, the realm of the cross-over between the theory of experience and the theory of freedom, it is just as imperative that this transformation not end up in a confounding of freedom and experience, even though the concept of experience may be changed in the metaphysical realm by the concept of freedom in a sense that is perhaps as yet unknown," ("On the Program of the Coming Philosophy," 7).

55. "The Task of the Translator," in *Illuminations*, 77.

56. Other examples of the rhetoric of the task appear in the artwork essay and "The Storyteller," *GS* 1: 504–5 and 2: 464–65, respectively.

57. See also the early (probably 1918) fragment, "Die Unendliche Aufgabe," *GS* 6: 51–52. The Kantian concept of the endless task drew Benjamin's attention as part of his dissertation work. He writes, "But where does the endless task lie if it cannot be given? It lies in science *(Wissenschaft)* itself, or rather it *is* this science. The unity of science depends not on being the answer to an endless question but that it cannot be ascertained," *GS* 6: 51. See also the editors' notes, *GS* 6:663–65.

58. *GS* 4: 21.

59. *GS* 2: 367. Benjamin also recounts the legend in his proposal for a journal called *Angelus Novus, GS* 2: 246.

60. *GS* 2: 464–65.

61. Ibid.

62. "Theses," in *Illuminations*, 257–58. See also the "Theologico-Political Fragment," in *Reflections*, 312–13.

63. *GS* 2: 212–13, 2: 178–79, and 1: 704, respectively.

64. See "Der Sürrealismus," *GS* 2: 307.

65. See discussion in chapter 5, below.

66. See Otto Eissfeldt, *Das Lied Moses Deuteronomium 32:1–34 und Das Lehrgedicht Asaphs Psalm 78 Samt Einer Analyse der Umbegung des Mose-Liedes* (Berlin: Akademie-Verlag, 1958). Although Eissfeldt dates Ps. 78 later than the Song of Moses and the label *maskîl* may significantly postdate both texts, the heavy use of wisdom vocabulary, including the verb *skl* in v. 29, along with the parallels to Ps. 78, suggests it is possible to view Deut. 32 as either a *shîr* or *maskîl*.

67. *GS* 5: 574.

68. "Karl Kraus" (1931), in *Reflections*, 269. See chapter 4 for more discussion of this essay.

CHAPTER 4

# The Bible in the Modern World

> If you had to speak quickly, standing on one leg, as Hillel the
> Jewish teacher of antiquity once did, the sentence would go:
> "The earth belongs only to those who live from the powers of
> the cosmos." Nothing distinguishes ancient from modern peo-
> ple as much as their abandonment of cosmic experience, which
> moderns hardly know.[1]

$M$ost contemporary notions of sacred text are confessional: they focus on how individuals and communities affirm the sacred status of literature, usually on internalist grounds. Such views usually focus on conscious belief and action: individuals affirm the sacred status of texts by writing, reciting, and interpreting them according to well-articulated traditions. These accounts place sacred texts in the category of creeds: one either adopts or rejects a text's sacred status, a decision that significantly determines personal and communal religious identity.

But texts and traditions work in other ways as well. We do not choose the time or place of our birth, and we do not choose the sacred texts that shape our culture. The Bible permeates law, litera-ture, thought, and action for all inheritors of Western tradition, and it exerts this influence in its capacity as sacred text. Benjamin's view of the Bible as a sacred text takes modern culture and the diversity of religious communities into account.[2]

Benjamin views the Bible as a sacred text within a theory of language and contemporary culture. This notion does not distin-guish a priori between sacred and nonsacred texts. The thesis that the Bible is a sacred text in contemporary Western culture does not deny that other texts may likewise be understood. That few texts have had comparable influence on Western history and culture is undeniable, but whether the Bible differs in degree or in kind from other texts is a question for a definitional theory of sacred text. As Benjamin sees Western philosophy and literature, the Bible is an archive of pure language and the paradigm of the scriptural function. Following a brief survey of contemporary views of the Hebrew Bible, this chapter discusses Benjamin's view in the intellectual context of his early work, with emphasis on the work of Martin Buber and Franz Rosenzweig.

## The Bible in Biblical Studies

Biblical scholarship underwent a radical transformation in the nineteenth century. The advent and refinement of historical and archaeological research increasingly called into question Church teachings about the date, authority, and history of the Bible. The most influential of these developments was the documentary hypothesis of Julius Wellhausen. In his *Prolegomena zur Geschichte Israels* (1878), Wellhausen divided the Pentateuch into four documentary sources: J, E, D, and P. For Wellhausen, "The Torah in its entirety is no longer the norm; *it has been replaced by the historical process that produced it.*"[3] The theory of biblical sources thus undermined the traditional authority of the Bible. A second influential development in modern biblical scholarship was the form-critical approach developed by Hermann Gunkel. According to this view, biblical texts can be divided into various genres *(Gattungen),* and each genre corresponds to a particular socio-religious context *(Sitz im Leben).*[4] For Gunkel, the tasks of historical critical scholarship thus become isolating each genre in its pure form and reconstructing its "place in life" in the early Israelite community. Like Wellhausen's documentary hypothesis, this approach tended to privilege early forms of religious practice over the canonical version of the Bible. While form criticism contributed new ways of understanding the history and function of biblical texts, such as the importance of the oral traditions predating the redacted biblical text, its clear debt to German idealist thought and the lack of evidence to support its claims have sharply diminished its influence in contemporary biblical studies.[5] Like the documentary hypothesis, form critical research opened new avenues for biblical studies and questioned the authority of the Masoretic Text. But the attempt to identify the *Gattung* and the *Sitz im Leben* behind the biblical text remained a matter of controversy and speculation.

A third important development in biblical studies has been the contribution of archaeology. Under William Albright and his followers, most notably Frank Cross, scholars have sought support for biblical traditions in the concrete findings of archaeological research. These scholars claim that artifacts and documents found by archaeologists corroborate the historicity of the Bible and "provide a source of material external to the Bible which can be used as a control against the unnecessary dependency upon literary, philosophical, or fundamentalist hypotheses."[6] More recently, however, scholars have questioned the entire enterprise of biblical archaeology, citing such controversial cases as the historicity of the Israelite conquest of Jericho.[7] Far from corroborating the Bible with archaeology as Albright had hoped, biblical archaeology in many cases further undermined the Bible's historicity.

A fourth trend in biblical studies, the canonical criticism developed by Brevard Childs, "focuses its attention on the final form of the text itself."[8] Without denying the findings of historical and archaeological studies, canonical criticism isolates the corpus of writings that were taken by Israel to be normative at a particular time. For Childs, the Hebrew Bible constitutes this canon because of its normative status as divine revelation for the community of ancient Israel. Against those historical critics who insist that the earliest source is the most authoritative, canonical criticism bases the normativity of the Hebrew Bible on its authoritative function for the religious community.

Childs claims that canonical criticism is primarily descriptive,[9] yet the basis of his decision to choose a certain period of ancient Israel and a certain collection of texts remains unclear. Earlier periods of ancient Israelite history canonized other texts, and later periods included midrash and the Talmud in the body of sacred literature. Despite his professed antipathy toward biblical theology,[10] the only justification Childs provides for the study of the canonical text is theological.[11] Canonical criticism recovers the authority of the Hebrew Bible, but it does so primarily on Protestant theological grounds.[12]

All four methods discussed above address the status of the Hebrew Bible. The documentary hypothesis, form criticism, and archaeological studies all shift the focus from the final text to other phenomena, leaving the status of the Bible itself unclear if not questioned. Jon Levenson comments that "[h]istorical critics take the text apart more ruthlessly than traditional *pashtanim,* and *qua* historical critics, they lack a method of putting it back together again."[13] Canonical criticism, on the other hand, attempts to reestablish the authority of the final text, but this position is available chiefly to members of Childs's religious community.

Thus, the challenge facing scholars who study the Bible in its final form is to explain the status of the Bible for biblical studies and contemporary culture in general. If the Bible is not merely a historical datum, and if it has significance for many different religious communities, then it must be possible to describe its status for contemporary Western culture in general. To view the Bible as merely a literary text or a relic of history without acknowledging its status in contemporary Western culture is to avoid the history and significance of biblical studies itself.

## *Benjamin, Buber, and Rosenzweig*

The historical–critical, theological, and literary schools of biblical studies all provide a limited account of the Hebrew Bible as a sacred text. These approaches appeal either to the claims of a single religious community or to elaborations of the text's internal claims. What is needed instead is a conceptual account of the Bible as a sacred text in contemporary culture.

There are significant affinities between the notion of sacred text in the Bible (Deuteronomy 31–34) and Benjamin's philosophy. Both involve a progression toward sacred texts that combines ideal past with imperfect present and *traditum* with *traditio;* both develop a model of sacred texts through innovative compositional methods. The heteroglot text of Deuteronomy 31–34 represents sacred texts both as the replacement of and testimony to the leadership of Moses. Benjamin's philosophical practice gestures toward a lost ideal and mimetic language without claiming to recover it.

The Bible reveals a surprising compositional and semantic rich-
ness and openness to multiple interpretations. In Deuteronomy
31–34, the variety of literary forms and texts and the open-ended
reference of *torah* (as law, song, and even life) distinguish it as a
composition that addresses the issue of sacred texts in a sophisti-
cated and far-reaching way and one that complements Benjamin's
notion of sacred text.

The central difference between the ideas of sacred text in the
Bible and in Benjamin's writings involves religious community. The
Bible addresses members of specific religious communities and
their descendants. In this sense, sacred text simply denotes a text
construed by a religious community to have particular religious
significance, through its content or authorship, for the members
of that community. In the Bible, texts are read out loud and in public,
usually for instructive or ritual purposes of the community.[14] Private
reading for pleasure or personal edification is alien to the Bible.[15]

For Benjamin, public reading has either disappeared or degenerated into consumerism; the religious community is replaced by
individual readers; and writing has suffered a comparable fate.[16] At
the same time, post-Biblical writing symbolizes and thus allows
glimpses of pure language. Direct revelation has become impossible,
but through strategies of writing and interpreting such as translation, quotation, juxtaposed genres, and the rhetoric of the task,
reading and writing regain meaning.

In order to place Benjamin's thought in its intellectual context,
this discussion compares his work with two German–Jewish con-
temporaries whose views on language and the Hebrew Bible developed independently of Benjamin's: Martin Buber and Franz
Rosenzweig. Like many other Jewish intellectuals in pre–Nazi Germany, Buber and Rosenzweig worked within the broad context of
German intellectual culture.[17] Like Benjamin, they brought their
general philosophical and philological training to bear on the emerging rebirth of Jewish intellectual culture in Germany.

In addition to doing this century's most significant work in
Jewish philosophy and theology, Buber and Rosenzweig also col-
laborated on a translation of the Hebrew Bible into German primarily for German-speaking Jews. In the course of this process, both
wrote essays reflecting on the philosophical and theological dimen-

sions of the project, collected in the volume *Die Schrift und ihre Verdeutschung.*[18] The essays contain insights into their conceptions of language, translation, and sacred text and display remarkable affinities with Benjamin's independently developed early thought.

Martin Buber represents the most influential and creative intellectual voice in twentieth-century German Jewry. His Jewish revival of the early 1900s addressed the issues of Jewish identity through the cultivation among a growing circle of intellectuals of historical, cultural, philosophical, and theological writings. This broader intellectual movement, together with Buber's own philosophy, had a significant impact on German-Jewish intellectuals and leaders, including Walter Benjamin.[19] Buber's influence, which first appears in Benjamin's work in 1912, challenged every German–Jewish intellectual to consider the issues of Jewish identity and Zionism.[20] Benjamin's letters to Ludwig Strauss respond with the idea of "cultural Zionism."[21]

Benjamin's cultural and intellectual conception of his Jewish identity led eventually to a confrontation with Buber. For Benjamin, Buber represented to some extent the authority of an established and influential new movement among German–Jewish intellectuals, and their early dialogue was broken off by Benjamin in 1916, when he reacted negatively to a request from Buber to contribute to the journal *Der Jude.* Benjamin seized this opportunity to elaborate his own ideas of language in opposition to what he characterized (unfairly) as Buber's notion of language as a pure means *(blosse Mittel)* from word to action:

> In this sense language is therefore only a means to the more or less suggestive preparation for motives which determine enterprises in the inner soul ... Every enterprise, which lies in the expansive tendency of word-to-word lines, seems to me dreadful and so much more disastrous where this entire relation of word to action extends, as with us, in always-increasing mass, as a mechanism for the realization of true absolutes.[22]

That such a characterization of Buber's thought was unfair and based on a more specific disagreement on the political position of German–Jewish intellectuals on World War I cannot be denied, but at the same time it can be said that there were deep differences between the two philosophers' views. Buber's emphasis on the individual's direct encounter with the Jewish tradition stood in stark contrast to Benjamin's interest in a broad analysis of modern culture as a nonobservant, intellectual Jew.

At the same time, there are important affinities between their notions of language and the Bible that in other circumstances might have produced a fruitful dialogue and even collaboration. The most important source for this comparison is *Die Schrift und ihre Verdeutschung.* For Buber, language, especially the language of the Hebrew Bible, is a spoken utterance linked both to creation and revelation (the divine–human dialogue).[23] Grete Schaeder describes Buber's conceptions of the Bible and language in theological and humanist terms:

> Language in its sensible spiritual double nature is the real mark of our humanity and unique creation; it is the receptacle of divine Revelation: "Humanism moves from the mystery of language to the mystery of the human person. The reality of language must become operative in a man's spirit. The truth of language must prove itself in a person's existence. That was the intent of humanistic education, so long as it was alive." The creative powers of antiquity have been preserved and transmitted by means of language. The native vigor of Hebrew humanity has come down to us in the biblical word which can still move us to spiritual restoration.[24]

Like Buber, Benjamin (in his 1916 essay on language) linked language in general and the Bible in particular to the theological categories of creation and revelation.[25] For Benjamin, however, the pure language of creation and revelation evades human experience after the Fall.[26] Accordingly, while Buber situated the translation, interpretation, and study of the Hebrew Bible at the center of his Hebrew humanism, Benjamin dedicated himself to the task of uncovering the factors that in his view obstructed the modern experience of the Bible as pure language of revelation.

Buber explains the function of modern biblical study in his 1926 essay "The Man of Today and the Jewish Bible":

The man of today knows of no beginning. As far as he is concerned, history ripples toward him from some prehistorical cosmic age. He knows of no end; history sweeps him on into a posthistorical cosmic age. . . . Man of today resists the Scriptures because he cannot endure revelation. . . . Man of today resists the Scriptures because he no longer wants to accept responsibility. He thinks he is venturing a great deal, yet he industriously evades the one real venture, that of responsibility.[27]

In modern times, Buber claims, "the spirit imposes no obligations"; for the modern intellectual, "Everything except everyday life belongs to the realm of the spirit."[28] There is a split in modern life between spirit and reality, even for those who recognize the importance of the spirit, a problem leading in his view either to "spurious idealism" or "spurious realism."[29]

In Buber's view, the challenge to modern man is to reunite reality with spirit, and the best response to this challenge is the return to the Hebrew Bible as a means of returning religion to reality.[30] The "man of today" may undertake a program of reading the Jewish Bible "as though it were something entirely unfamiliar."[31] The task is a difficult one requiring personal strength of will: "This terrifying world is the world of God. It lays claim upon you. Prove yourself in it as a man of God!"[32] In this way, Buber claims, the man of today can recover a true understanding of history, beginnings, and personal meaning through the biblical categories of creation, revelation, and redemption.

The Hebrew Bible is thus a restorative for the man of today, reconciling the modern split between spirit (i.e., religion) and reality, with the result that the man of today who encounters the Bible can achieve a meaningful understanding of self and history to replace the spurious idealisms and spurious realisms prevalent in contemporary culture. The details of what accounts for the modern situation remain sketchy, as well as the mechanism whereby the Bible acts on the man of today.

Benjamin had a different assessment of the status of the Bible in contemporary culture. Although he held some views about language and the Bible in common with Buber, he disagreed with Buber's assessment of modernity and with the accessibility of the

Bible to the modern man through force of personal will. Benjamin tentatively agreed with Sigfried Kracauer's critical review of the Buber and Rosenzweig translation, which judged the entire project and its language to be anachronistic.[33] Claiming that only one translation—Luther's—could render the Bible into German, Kracauer calls the translation "romantic and arbitrary," arguing, "For today access to truth is by way of the profane."[34] Benjamin's letter to Scholem takes a more cautious position, but shares Kracauer's emphasis on the timing of the translation:

> I don't need to say that I do not see myself, much less Kracauer, as competent in this matter. I can only speculate about something to which I have no tactical access (which I cannot touch), rather only from a distance and from one direction—above— from the mass of the German *Sprachgeist.* I have no idea who or what in the whole world a translation of the Bible into the German of our times could properly concern. Just now, when the contents of Hebrew are newly realized, German for its part is at a highly problematic stage, and given all the fruitful links between the two in general, which seem only latent to me, doesn't this translation come down to a questionable display of affairs which, being put on show, instantly repudiate themselves in light of this German?[35]

Despite its inquisitive stance, the letter plainly doubts the cultural value of Buber and Rosenzweig's translation.[36] Like Kracauer, Benjamin sees contemporary culture as rife with and dependent upon the sacred text of the Bible even while profoundly alienated from it. In *One-Way Street,* he contrasts Luther's time, when the translation of the "book of books" triumphantly appeared, to the present, in which books face extinction.[37] As a philosopher of culture, Benjamin situates the Bible in a position at once more influential (through cultural phenomena) and less accessible through personal effort than Buber does.

The philosophical affinities between the thought of Franz Rosenzweig and Benjamin are more striking than those between Benjamin and Buber. While the influence of Rosenzweig on Benjamin's later work has been discussed at length elsewhere,[38] my purpose lies in outlining some points of contact between the early work of the two in the areas of linguistic philosophy, translation, and the contemporary status of the Bible.

For Rosenzweig and Benjamin, language is linked directly to thought and therefore enables them to speak of language *in general,* the unity of language, and the centrality of translation to linguistic philosophy. In "Die Schrift und Luther" (1926), Rosenzweig writes:

> There is only one language—with this paradox I sought to grasp, in another treatment of the problem of translation ["Die Schrift und das Wort"—1925], all at once the task, the end as the way. This unity of all languages is more deeply hidden for their elementary element, the word, than for their complete element, the sentence.[39]

Because sentences express thought, they expose the unity and translatability of languages more clearly than words. Like Benjamin, Rosenzweig considers the practice of translation to be an illustration of the unity of languages. Rosenzweig's and Benjamin's notions of language and linguistic unity justify the possibility of translation and form the basis of a general philosophy (and theology) of language.

If there is one original language, as both thinkers suggest, then it becomes necessary to explain the diversity of languages in history. For Rosenzweig, as for Benjamin, the theological categories of creation and revelation explain the division between the originary unity of language and the current plurality of tongues. Rosenzweig describes original language as "archetypal language" in *The Star of Redemption* (1919):

> Those inaudible elemental words, standing side by side without relationship, were the language of the individual elements of the protocosmos, lying side by side. They were the language which is understood in the soundless realm of the Faustian Mothers, no more than the ideational possibilities of arriving at an understanding. Real language, however, is the language of the terrestrial world. The language of logic is the prognostica-

tion of this real language of grammar. Reasoning is mute in each individual by himself, yet common to all.[40]

On a structural level, the linguistic philosophies of Benjamin and Rosenzweig are quite close: the original unity of language, linked to theologies of creation and revelation, precedes (though not in simple chronological terms) the plurality of languages.[41] The substance of their theories, however, differs; while Rosenzweig emphasizes human speech and a fusion of reason and belief, Benjamin places the category of the text and a suspicion of both reason and belief at the center of his philosophy of language.[42]

If the diversity of languages emerges from an essential linguistic unity, then translation must not only be possible but also a privileged form of linguistic practice, and for Rosenzweig and Benjamin, translation functions both as a key philosophical category and as an important activity. In language that closely parallels Benjamin's translation essay, Rosenzweig writes in *Star* that,

> Through the miracle of language, speech overcomes the resistance of the today that once was, and though separated by language, still is as of today. It is the first effect of the spirit to translate, to erect a bridge between man and man, between tongue and tongue. The Bible must surely be the first book to be translated and then held equal to the original translation. God speaks everywhere with the words of men.[43]

Like Benjamin, Rosenzweig links translation to revelation, the underlying unity of language, and more remarkably, to the Bible as the document whose translation gains the status of the original because of its status as sacred text.[44] Both Benjamin and Rosenzweig rank translation among the most important human activities: "The true goal of the mind," writes Rosenzweig, "is translating."[45] Translation is only possible because of the essential unity of languages, and the chief illustration of this fundamental truth is the sacred text of the Bible.

The Bible and its translation represent not mere facts but central philosophical categories for Benjamin and Rosenzweig. The original unity of language lies for both in the language of creation and revelation, and thus the Bible, as receptacle of revelation par excellence, lends itself most readily to translation, which is simply the bridging of different languages according to their underlying unity. The convergences between Rosenzweig and Benjamin seem remarkable not only because they worked independently but also because of the striking differences between their views. In general, these convergences can be explained by a common philosophical (and theological) tradition, which I illustrate through a discussion of Hamann and Humboldt. Their main point of divergence, on the other hand, lies in the area of epistemology,[46] specifically in their estimation of contemporary rationality. This difference becomes clearer in the following discussion of the influences of Hamann and Humboldt on Rosenzweig and Benjamin.

Johann Georg Hamann (1730–88) identified language as the central constituent of human nature and the key to religious philosophy:

> Every natural being is a word of God through which He speaks to man. The real meeting between God and man, however, takes place in the world of history: nature and history are for Hamann "the two great Commentaries of the divine Word, which is the only key capable of disclosing their meaning to us."[47]

The influence of Hamann's philosophy of language on Rosenzweig and Benjamin can be seen most clearly with respect to two categories: poetry and translation. In "Aesthetica in Nuce," Hamann traces the origins of language to poetry and biblical creation: "Poetry is the mother tongue *(Muttersprache)* of the human race."[48] On translation, Hamann proclaims, "Discourse *(Reden)* is translation—from an angelic language into a human language, which means thoughts into words, things into names, pictures into signs."[49] Hamann's originality lies not so much in his linkage of poetry to scripture as his emphasis on poetic and sacred language as conceptual foundations of language in general. Hamann's theory of language functioned chiefly as a critique of rationalist critical philosophy.

Though Benjamin and Rosenzweig both inherited the linguistic legacy of Hamann, they adapted it in different ways. While "Aesthetica in Nuce" appears to privilege poetry over prose and equates it with scripture, Rosenzweig asserts the priority of scriptural prose over poetry: "The Bible is the shelter of this human language, because it is prose. . . . All poetry is inspired *(begeistert)* by the spirit of prose."[50] With Hamann, Rosenzweig positions language at the center of philosophy in place of reason as conceived by Enlightenment thinkers; but while Hamann's linguistic theory can be described as aesthetic–theological (as primarily Christian theology), Rosenzweig's linguistic theory can be characterized more as theological–ethical (as primarily Jewish theology). Rosenzweig took exception not only to the rationalism of Kant (as Hamann did), but also to the supersession of theology (and Judaism) posited by Hegel.[51] Rosenzweig's theory of language, with the spoken word of revelation at its core, revises Hamann's theory in theological terms.

Hamann's legacy took a different turn in Benjamin's work, following epistemological rather than theological lines. Like Hamann and Rosenzweig, Benjamin believed that a true understanding of language lay at the center of philosophy and theology,[52] and that it was possible to distinguish between originary and secondary forms of language, like Hamann's priority of poetry as *Muttersprache* over rationalist prose and Rosenzweig's distinction between archetypal words and real words.[53]

Benjamin, like Hamann and Rosenzweig, describes the origins of language in terms of biblical creation, but for Benjamin the pure language of Adam lies virtually beyond the epistemological scope of humanity after the Fall. According to Benjamin, the language accessible to us is only a shell of the pure, mimetic language that preceded it.[54] It thus becomes impossible to encounter or recover originary language under contemporary conditions, except for the brief moments of "shock" or "profane illumination" afforded by the kind of critical work, including commentary and translation, he proposes.[55] Benjamin's persistent interest in allegory and the transmutation of religious phenomena in early modern culture reflects the view that only a critical understanding of contemporary language and culture can afford a glimpse of pure language.

The conception—shared by Benjamin and Rosenzweig—that language is the primary medium for thought can be traced to Wilhelm von Humboldt. More than Hamann and Herder, Humboldt sought to develop a general theory of language from a philosophical and philological standpoint. Central to his work is the tension between language as convention and language as the natural, essential bridge between subject and object, thought and world.[56] While Rosenzweig was particularly sympathetic to Hamann's "kabbalistic" quest for a *Muttersprache*, Benjamin shares Humboldt's interest in the philosophical study of contemporary language. Thus, although Humboldt's work is less explicitly theological than Hamann's, it plays a greater role in Benjamin's philosophy of language and sacred text.

Notwithstanding their similar views of language, translation, and Scripture, Benjamin and Rosenzweig differed in their respective views of the Bible as a sacred text in contemporary culture. Rosenzweig wrote (in 1929):

> It is quite possible that the secularization of religious communities, which began a hundred and fifty years ago, will march on, and that church and synagogue in the old traditional sense will persist only for a small nucleus, while a worldly agent, the "church people" or, in our case, the "Jewish people," will become the general community. If this should take place, the significance of the Holy Scriptures would not lessen but would even grow.... When dogma and Law cease to be the all-embracing frame of the community and serve only as props from within, the Scriptures must not merely fulfil the tasks of all Scriptures: to establish a connection between generations; they must also assume another which is likewise incumbent on all Scriptures: they must guarantee the connection between the center and periphery of the community. Thus, even if church and synagogue no longer arched the portal on the road of humanity, the Bible would still continue to be at beck and call, so that humanity would consult it about this very road, "turn its pages again and again," and find "everything in it."[57]

With this, Rosenzweig separates the significance of the Bible from institutionalized religion, and at the same time, he affirms its status as Holy Scripture for humanity in general. For even the modern person, who both believes and doubts, "belongs to" the Scriptures.[58]

In Rosenzweig's theological–philosophical vision, the Bible represents the central categories of creation, revelation, archetypal word, speech, and translation.[59] And despite the secularization of modern culture, the Bible remains for Rosenzweig an accessible text because, he claims in a move at once Hegelian and rabbinical, it encompasses humanity in some significant way. This final move represents the main difference between Benjamin and Rosenzweig on language and sacred texts; Benjamin hesitates to characterize the Bible as accessible in contemporary culture, even though he views it as equally foundational in philosophical and theological terms.

Both Benjamin and Rosenzweig understood the Bible to be philosophically and linguistically crucial to modern life despite the secularization of contemporary culture. But while Rosenzweig (together with Buber) developed a novel program of biblical translation and reinterpretation for modern German-speaking Jews, Benjamin avoided study and analysis of the Bible because he remained skeptical of its epistemological accessibility (as sacred text and pure language) to contemporary understanding. "The Bible, in regarding itself as a revelation, must necessarily evolve the fundamental linguistic facts," he wrote, but these facts evade the immediate grasp of modern experience.[60]

This divergence between Benjamin and Rosenzweig emerges, I think, from two deeper differences in their thought. First, Rosenzweig (like Buber) identifies language and scripture primarily as speech, while Benjamin consistently refers to the Bible as *text* (see chapter 5). Secondly, while Rosenzweig mentions the secularization of culture as a fact of history that leaves the sacred status of scripture untouched, Benjamin complicates the opposition of sacred and profane with a model of modernity in which the category of the sacred is more likely to appear indirectly, in allegory and ostensibly non-religious texts (see chapter 6). Stéphane Mosès expresses this difference in terms of communication: "[T]he communicative function of language, which for Benjamin represents the main symptom of its degeneration, is for Rosenzweig identical with its quality of revelation."[61]

The most obvious difference between Benjamin and Rosenzweig (and Buber) with respect to the Bible is that the latter studied and translated the Bible while Benjamin spoke of it only in passing without sustained analysis. This difference reflects not dilettantism on Benjamin's part, as his patient study of nonbiblical literature shows, but rather the importance of the Bible to him as a philosophical category, a linguistic horizon at once informing and at the same time evading modern experience and understanding.[62] Benjamin's interest in the allegories of German *Trauerspiel*, Baudelaire, and modern avant-garde art lay largely in how these phenomena of modern and premodern culture manifested the persistence and transformation of the sacred.[63]

Benjamin's position varies from Buber and Rosenzweig less on the question of the linguistic-philosophical nature of the Bible than in the assessment of contemporary culture in relation to the Bible. For Buber and Rosenzweig, the modern situation is characterized by the shift from sacred to profane history understood mainly in theological terms: modern history is profane history alienated from the sacred, and the Hebrew Bible represents a pathway back to the sacred. Buber and Rosenzweig conceived of the Bible as a primary source of revelation for humanity in an age of secularization. Benjamin, however, described modernity in more epistemological terms: modern history is not so much profane history (for sacred phenomena continue to persist, though often in disguise) as it is a condition in which language and thought have degenerated from unity to multiplicity and from symbolic name to abstract communication.[64] This condition cannot be relieved by direct appeal to the Hebrew Bible but rather must begin with a critical evaluation of the contemporary standpoint from which the Bible is approached.

Rosenzweig's characterization of modernity and the Bible, as shown above, resembles Buber's, even though his theory of language and Scripture comes close to Benjamin's. Buber and Rosenzweig developed Jewish theology and philosophy as solutions to the modern alienation from the Bible as sacred text, while Benjamin undertook a critical philosophy that scrutinizes the categories of sacred and profane history and texts. His notion of modernity, fully developed in his later work on Baudelaire and the Paris Arcades, is a state of alienation from pure language that is nevertheless capable of "profane illumination" through critical philosophy.

Benjamin saw the Bible both as a receptacle of pure language and as a narrative of its loss.[65] While Buber and Rosenzweig moved in the direction of existential and philosophical theology and a primarily internalist view of the Bible's status, Benjamin gravitated toward a critical epistemology and historiography that both preserve and revise the idea of the Bible as a sacred text in contemporary culture.

In his *Trauerspiel* study, Benjamin identifies Adam as "the father of the human race and the father of philosophy": "Adam's action of naming things is so far removed from play or caprice that it actually confirms the state of paradise as a state in which there is as yet no need to struggle with the communicative significance of words."[66] The opposition between the pure, symbolic language of names and the fallen, communicative language of history (and abstraction) summarizes Benjamin's theory of language; it is the task of philosophy, he claims, "to restore, by representation, the primacy of the symbolic character of the word."[67] Though he later modified his philosophical methods, this purpose arguably underlies much of Benjamin's writing, especially through his interest in baroque and modern allegory. Benjamin characterizes allegory, and all sacred writings, as representing the antimonies of profane and sacred, openness and closure, multiple signs and single complex: "The desire to guarantee the sacred character of any script—there will always be a conflict between sacred standing and profane comprehensibility—leads to complexes, to hieroglyphics."[68]

In the world of historical languages, sacred texts, including the Hebrew Bible, lie between the Adamic language of naming and the fallen language of communication. Their status in contemporary culture cannot be explained solely in internalist or externalist terms, but rather only through a theory that overcomes this opposition: the tree of the sacred text is sustained by the leaves of commentary and translation, but these leaves have no vitality without the sacred text. As a sacred text, the Bible approaches the symbolic, naming language of Adam, but as a text written and studied in the language of history, it remains understandable primarily as communication and the representation of the loss of pure language. This view, which is developed in the following chapter, parallels the biblical dynamics of openness and closure, instruction *(torah)* and artifact *('ed)*, text and life.

NOTES

1. *GS* 4: 146.

2. See Fishbane, "The Notion of Sacred Text," in *The Garments of Torah*, 121–31.

3. Jon Levenson, "The Hebrew Bible, The Old Testament, and Historical Criticism," in *The Future of Biblical Studies: The Hebrew Scriptures*, ed. R. Friedman and H. Williamson, Semeia Studies (Decatur, GA: Scholars Press, 1987), 35.

4. Martin J. Buss, "The Study of Forms," in *Old Testament Form Criticism*, ed. John H. Hayes (San Antonio: Trinity University Press, 1974), 51–53.

5. A more recent practitioner of form criticism, Gerhard von Rad, made important contributions to biblical studies, but in his attempt to reconstruct the religious background of the Pentateuch, he tried unsuccessfully to conform their discoveries to preformulated theological and historical categories. See Brevard Childs, *Introduction to the Old Testament as Scripture* (Philadelphia: Fortress, 1979), 120–21. Also see Gerhard von Rad's theological claims in *Old Testament Theology* (New York: Harper and Row, 1965).

6. John Hayes, "The History of the Study of Israelite and Judaean History," in *Israelite and Judaean History*, ed. John Hayes and J. Maxwell Miller (Philadelphia: Westminster, 1977), 66.

7. J. Maxwell Miller, "The Israelite Occupation of Canaan," in *Israelite and Judaean History*, 256.

8. Brevard Childs, *Introduction to the Old Testament as Scripture* (Philadelphia: Fortress, 1979), 73.

9. Ibid., 72.

10. See Childs, *Biblical Theology in Crisis* (Philadelphia: Fortress, 1970).

11. "However, apart from unintentional bias which is always present to some extent, the religious stance of the modern reader can play a legitimate role after the descriptive task has been accomplished, when the reader chooses whether or not to identify with the perspectives of the canonical texts of Israel which he has studied." Childs, *Introduction to the Old Testament as Scripture*, 72–73.

12. As James Barr has shown in *Holy Scripture* (Westminster: Philadelphia, 1983), 132–39. Claiming that canonical criticism "liberates from the stifling effect of academic scholasticism," Childs blurs the Bible's authority for ancient Israel with its authority for contemporary believers:

> [T]he interpreter is forced to confront the authoritative text of scripture in a continuing theological reflection. By placing the canonical text within the context of the community of faith and practice a variety of different exegetical models are freed to engage the text, such as the liturgical or the dramatic. Childs, *Introduction*, 83.

Childs shifts uncritically between the authority of the Bible for Israel, a question of historical analysis that he treats only summarily, and the authority of the Bible for contemporary Christians, a theological position that contradicts his claim to descriptive neutrality.

13. Levenson, "The Hebrew Bible," in *The Future of Biblical Studies: The Hebrew Scriptures*, 20.

14. Daniel Boyarin, "Placing Reading: Ancient Israel and Medieval Europe," in *The Ethnography of Reading*, Jonathan Boyarin, ed. (Berkeley: University of California Press, 1993), 13.

15. Ibid., p. 19.

16. See *One-Way Street*, in *Reflections*, esp. pp. 66 and 77. Note also that the heading over the passage on sacred and profane texts reads, "To the Public: Please Protect and Preserve These Plantings," p. 67.

17. See George L. Mosse, *German Jews beyond Judaism* (Bloomington: Indiana University Press, 1985).

18. Buber and Rosenzweig, *Die Schrift und ihre Verdeutschung* (Berlin: Schocken, 1936).

19. See Anson Rabinbach, "Between Enlightenment and Apocalypse: Benjamin, Bloch and Modern German Jewish Messianism," *New German Critique* 34 (1985): 88–89.

20. Ibid., 89–96.

21. Letter of October 10, 1912, *GS* 2: 838.

22. *Briefe*, 1: 126.

23. See Michael Fishbane, "The Biblical Dialogue of Martin Buber," in *The Garments of Torah*, 81–90.

24. Grete Schaeder, *The Hebrew Humanism of Martin Buber*, trans. Noah J. Jacobs (Detroit: Wayne State University, 1973), 371. See the late essay, "The Word That Is Spoken," where Buber elaborates the dialogic and revelatory character of language: "[I]t is through God's addressing man—Franz Rosenzweig's *Stern der Erlösung* teaches us—that He establishes man in speech. A precommunicative state of language is unthinkable." *The Knowledge of Man: A Philosophy of the Interhuman*, trans. Maurice Friedman and Ronald G. Smith (New York: Harper and Row, 1965), 115. He also claims there that "[t]he ambiguity of the word, which we may call its aura, must to some measure already have existed whenever men in their multiplicity met each other, expressing this multiplicity in order not to succumb to it. It is the communal nature of the logos as at once 'word' and 'meaning' which makes man man, and it is this which proclaims itself from of old in the communalizing of the spoken word that again and again comes into being," 114–15.

25. "On Language," in *Reflections*, 314–32.

26. Ibid., 327–29.

27. Martin Buber, "The Man of Today and the Jewish Bible," in *On the Bible*, ed. Nahum Glatzer (New York: Schocken, 1982).

28. Ibid., 2.

29. Ibid., 2, 6.

30. Ibid., 3.

31. Ibid., 5.

32. Buber, "Biblical Humanism," in *On the Bible*, 216.

33. Letters to Scholem, May 29 and September 18, 1926, *Briefe* 1: 429, 432. The review, as well as a later response from Buber and Rosenzweig, and Kracauer's rebuttal to the response, appeared in *Frankfurter Zeitung*. "Die Bibel auf Deutsch," in *Das Ornament der Masse*, ed. Karsten Witte (Frankfurt: Suhrkamp Verlag, 1977), 173–86. The original review, along with Kracauer's later rebuttal to the response from Buber and Rosenzweig, is translated by Thomas Y. Levin in *The Mass Ornament* (Cambridge: Harvard University Press, 1995), 189–201.

34. Ibid., 200–201.

35. Ibid., 432.

36. Martin Jay notes the difference as follows: "Whereas Buber and Rosenzweig saw the Bible as an act of direct communication between a divine I and a human Thou, Benjamin minimized the importance of the receiving reader," "Politics of Translation: Siegfried Kracauer and Walter Benjamin on the Buber-Rosenzweig Bible," in *Permanent Exiles: Essays on the Intellectual Migration From Germany To America* (New York: Columbia University Press, 1985), 212.

37. *GS* 4: 102.

38. Stéphane Mosès, "Walter Benjamin and Franz Rosenzweig," in *Benjamin: Philosophy, History, Aesthetics*, ed. Gary Smith (Chicago: University of Chicago Press, 1989). See also Hennig Gunther, *Walter Benjamin und der Humane Marxismus* (Freiburg: Walter-Verlag, 1974), 46–52 and 70–71.

39. Franz Rosenzweig, "Die Schrift und Luther," in *Die Schrift und ihre Verdeutschung*, 124.

40. Franz Rosenzweig, *The Star of Redemption*, trans. W. Hallo (Notre Dame: Notre Dame Press, 1971), 109.

41. See "On Language," in *Reflections*, 319–30.

42. See, for example, Rosenzweig's *Star*, 366, and Benjamin's "Task of the Translator," in *Illuminations*, 77–82. See also Paul Mendes-Flohr, "Franz Rosenzweig's Concept of Philosophical Faith," *Leo Baeck Institute Year Book* 4 (London: Secker and Warburg, 1989), 357–69.

43. Rosenzweig, *The Star of Redemption*, 366.

44. See "The Task of the Translator," in *Illuminations*, 77–82.

45. Letter to Rudolf Ehrenberg, 1 October 1917, quoted in Everett Fox, "Franz Rosenzweig as Translator," *Leo Baeck Institute Yearbook* 34 (London, 1989), 379.

46. On Benjamin's epistemology, see Liselotte Wiesenthal, *Zur Wissenschaftstheorie Walter Benjamins* (Frankfurt: Athenäum, 1973).

47. Schaeder, *The Hebrew Humanism of Martin Buber*, 170.

48. Johann Georg Hamann, *Schriften zur Sprache*, ed. Josef Simon (Frankfurt: Suhrkamp, 1967), 107; see also references to Adam and divine creation, 110–14.

49. Johann Georg Hamann, "Aesthetica in Nuce," in *Schriften zur Sprache*, ed. Josef Simon (Frankfurt: Suhrkamp, 1967), 109.

50. Franz Rosenzweig, "Die Schrift und Das Wort," in *Die Schrift und ihre Verdeutschung*, 86–87. Cf. Benjamin's fragment on the messianic world, where history is written in a "liberated prose" *(befreite Prosa)* that "has broken the fetters of writing," *GS* 1: 1235.

51. Rosenzweig, *Star*, 107–9. See Mendes-Flohr, 358–59.

52. "On Language," in *Reflections*, 321.

53. Rosenzweig, *Star*, 109.

54. See Benjamin, "On the Mimetic Faculty," in *Reflections*, 333–36.

55. See the 1929 essay "Surrealism," in *Reflections*, 179, 190.

56. Wilhelm von Humboldt, "Über die Natur der Sprache im Allgemeinen," *Schriften zur Sprache*, 8–9.

57. Rosenzweig, "The Significance of the Bible in World History," in *Jewish Perspectives on Christianity*, ed. Fritz A. Rothschild (New York: Crossroad, 1990), 232.

58. Rosenzweig, "Die Schrift und Luther," in *Die Schrift und ihre Verdeutschung*, 109.

59. See Everett Fox, "Franz Rosenzweig as Translator," in *Leo Baeck Institute Year Book* (London: Secker and Warburg, 1989), 371–84.

60. "On Language," 322.

61. Stéphane Mosès, "Walter Benjamin and Franz Rosenzweig," in *Benjamin: Philosophy, History, Aesthetics*, 239.

62. See Benjamin's letter of August 11, 1934 to Gershom Scholem, *The Correspondence of Walter Benjamin and Gershom Scholem 1932–1940* (New York: Schocken, 1989), 134–36.

63. See Susan Buck-Morss, *The Dialectics of Seeing* (Cambridge, MA: MIT University Press, 1989), 247–52.

64. See *The Origin of German Tragic Drama*, 36, and "On Language," in *Reflections*.

65. See *The Origin of German Tragic Drama*, 233–34, and "On Language," in *Reflections*.

66. *The Origin of German Tragic Drama*, 36–37.

67. *The Origin of German Tragic Drama*, 36; see also "On Language" and "The Mimetic Faculty," in *Reflections*.

68. *The Origin of German Tragic Drama*, 175.

CHAPTER 5

# Benjamin's Biblical Interpretations

> I do not want to say more about the [Jewish] literary person
> as an idea other than that he is occupied in the new social
> consciousness, which is to be what "the poor in spirit, the
> oppressed, and the meek" were to the first Christians.[1]

*B*enjamin rarely refers to the Bible. With few exceptions, notably
the early essays on language and violence, he mentions the Bible
in passing, without extended commentary. But the idea of the Bible
as sacred text motivates his philosophy of language and the later
work on allegory and modernity. For Benjamin, the Bible represents
the paradigm of language (as speech and writing) and narration (as
story and history). Although he did not study the Bible and never
learned Hebrew, the Bible remains Benjamin's original narrative of
loss—it is the self-obscuring and self-effacing text behind the theories of language and history.

Nothing in Benjamin's writing indicates an intimate familiarity
with the Bible. Because he grew up in an assimilated Jewish family,
the Bible remained a distant reality that may paradoxically have
contributed to its special role in his work.[2] Though he did not
practice Judaism and rejected political Zionism, Benjamin took his
Jewish identity very seriously as the basis for his cultural and
intellectual work.[3] John McCole speaks of Benjamin's turn to Judaism as a part of a "new Jewish sensibility whose social and psychological roots lay partly in a vehement rejection of their parents'
assimilationist illusions":

> [A]fter the break with the youth movement, the terms of his
> balance between Jewish identity and work on German traditions
> shifted: he did not abandon his idealist commitments, but he

began to mobilize his Jewish identity in the process of recasting them. . . . The messianic idiom became one of the germs of what we might call an intellectual project or strategy—a radical but immanent critique of German idealism whose essential coordinates were already latent in his involvement in the youth movement.[4]

Benjamin's 1912 letter favoring "cultural Zionism" over political Zionism, and his break with Buber in 1916 confirm this vision.[5] The correspondence with Scholem also illustrates the important but unconventional role Judaism played in Benjamin's life. In a 1918 letter on Scholem's "Über Klage und Klagelied," for instance, Benjamin relates lament literature and the *Trauerspiel* to his Jewish identity.[6] Idealism, driven by the model of history as progress, led to nationalism. In his intellectual Zionism, Benjamin developed alternative ideas of history; these ideas—especially messianism—come from the Bible.[7] Despite his cultural Zionism, Benjamin's work is filled with references to Christianity. From the *Trauerspiel* study to the autobiographical writings, Christianity predominates. The casual references to the Bible in his letters are just as likely to mention Christ as the prophets.[8] The only biblical quotation in the translation essay comes—in Greek—from the New Testament: "In the beginning was the Word."[9] If Benjamin's project were simply to describe Western culture, the Christian emphasis would come as no surprise. The deeper problem lies in sorting out Benjamin's interpretive standpoint toward Christian sources. In this sense, Christianity—in the Bible, allegory, and European modernism—becomes the main locus for the critical study of the scriptural function. In keeping with his "cultural Zionism" and identity as a critic, Judaism represented for Benjamin more a set of interpretive strategies than a personal creed.

The portrayal of Christianity in Franz Rosenzweig's *The Star of Redemption* (1921) provides a fruitful comparison. For Rosenzweig, Christianity models historical time:

Thus Christianity gains mastery over time by making of the moment an epoch-making epoch. From Christ's birth on, there is henceforth only present. Time does not bounce off Christianity as it does off the Jewish people, but fugitive time has been arrested and must henceforth serve as a captive servant out of the present.[10]

Benjamin also sees the Christian Bible as the central force behind Western conceptions of history. It both establishes the quotidian structures of time and also points, through divine language and messianism, beyond history. But Christianity does not have the resources to reclaim pure language; that requires the critical practice of cultural Zionism. The "Theological-Political Fragment" makes a radical distinction between history and the messianic. Christianity creates history, but it takes Benjamin's critical Judaism, with its "weak messianic power," to see beyond history to a recovery of pure language and the messiah.[11]

There is thus a fundamental instability between Benjamin's attitude toward the Bible, which he sees both as a cultural form in Christendom and as the standpoint of critique in his intellectual Judaism. The Christian Bible and its legacy are the object of Benjamin's study as well as the basis for the philosophy of language and historiography. When he mentions the Bible or messianism, Benjamin rarely specifies the Hebrew Bible, but Jewish thought undeniably predominates, and he sometimes criticizes Christian anti-Semitism.[12] This ambivalence goes beyond critical method to the heart of Benjamin's project and perhaps his identity: Would there be room for a critique of Christendom and its modern legacy (including Baudelaire and surrealism as well as commodity culture) by means of a tradition shared by Christianity and Judaism?

This chapter surveys Benjamin's references to the Bible. The only extended interpretations of the Bible appear in the essays on language and violence. But there are other kinds of references to the Bible; these include brief mentions of the Bible and its figures, as well as indirect references through literature and theology. Despite their scarcity, these passages reveal Benjamin's persistent interest in the Bible, usually in relation to the following: linguistic philosophy, philosophy of religion, historiography, messianism, allegory, textuality, and modern literature and culture. A paradox runs through these references: as revelation, the Bible provides the basis for Western ideas of language, history, and culture, but as a textual archive of pure language, the Bible resists easy interpretation and postpones the recovery of pure language. Benjamin's avoidance of the Bible reinforces its importance to his work, for, as Rainer Nägele points out, "The authoritative claim of such texts as the Bible or 'Homer' is threatened by the all-too-simple appearance of their stories."[13] Just as human language symbolizes the lost mimetic function, the Bible symbolizes the loss of pure language.

## *The Book of Genesis in the Essay on Language (1916)*

The model of language as the communication of its own spiritual being emerges from the account of naming in Genesis. But the biblical account also narrates the deterioration of pure language, which engenders the language of the mere sign, judgment, and abstraction. This process is accompanied by the decline of the mimetic faculty, which develops into "nonsensuous similarity" in the archive of language, especially as writing. Benjamin identifies his objective as the restoration of pure language, but he considers this goal to be too ambitious for philosophy alone. He appeals instead to the form of language that most closely approximates the pure language of naming: sacred texts, specifically the Bible. But Benjamin does not undertake to write extensive biblical interpretations or commentary, because this method would only transform the Bible into mere signs and abstractions. Rather, he is interested in what the Bible reveals about itself as "ultimate reality, perceptible only in its manifestation, inexplicable and mystical." As revelation, the Bible "must necessarily evolve the fundamental linguistic facts," but these facts are only a philosophical representation of the spiritual being of the sacred text. Further, as a text, the Bible itself is only an archive of pure language, since it is written in a specific, historical language rather than spoken as name. As a sacred text, the Bible lies beyond the pure language it describes and represents, because the notion of sacred text implies the existence of profane texts; the dichotomy of sacred and profane is a condition of the Fall. Sacred texts are the archive of the pure language of naming, but they also represent its loss. The question with which Benjamin struggles, in these essays and in the *Trauerspiel* study, *Einbahn-*

*strasse,* and the *Passagen-Werk,* is how critical philosophy should characterize sacred texts in relation to the theory of language.

In the analysis of Genesis 1–2, there is a direct relation between divine language and divine creation: God says "let there be," God creates, and God names. Human language does not appear until the second creation story: "He did not wish to subject him to language, but in man God set language, which had served *Him* as medium of creation, free. God rested when he had left his creative power to itself in man. This creativity, relieved of its divine actuality, became knowledge."[14] A mimetic relationship, the making of man in God's image, accompanies the creation of human language. Human language constitutes

> only a reflection of the [divine creative] word in name. Name is no closer to the word than knowledge to creation. The infinity of all human language always remains limited and analytical in nature in comparison to the absolutely unlimited and creative infinity of the divine word.[15]

Human language only echoes the divine word of creation, even in naming, its highest form. Divine language is pure and creative, while human language is bourgeois, knowledge-based, and represented by mere signs. Language originally fits its objects mimetically, but with the multiplication of historical languages, objects become "overnamed" *(überbenannt)* and language becomes degraded and instrumentalized.[16]

This progressive decline becomes clearer with Benjamin's reading of Genesis 11. Before the Fall, human language is linked closely to divine creation, naming, and "spiritual being" *(geistige Wesen).*[17] "The Fall marks the birth of the *human word,* in which name no longer lives intact."[18] The human word communicates something other than itself; it becomes a "parody by the expressly mediate word of the expressly immediate."[19] After the Fall and the multiplication of languages at Babel, the pure language of naming gives way to the mere sign, the divine word of judgment, and abstraction.[20] First, by rejecting the "pure language of the name," language becomes a means *(Mittel)* and a mere sign *(blosse Zeichen).*[21] Second, the Fall precipitates the origin of a new kind of immediacy, the judging word, which has direct knowledge of good and evil and initiates punishment.[22] The third outcome of the Fall is abstraction, which entails a loss of communicative immediacy, the multiplicity and confusion of languages, and the condition in which "nature mourns" because its objects are "overnamed."[23]

In this fallen linguistic state (which corresponds to modernity), it is not clear what kind of linguistic activity is possible or desirable. But the essay itself, as an example of fallen language, provides an indication by combining two modes of discourse: an abstract, synchronic model of language in general, and a concrete, diachronic discussion of human language based on a biblical text. The essay begins with abstract philosophy, but it later becomes apparent that this model depends on the category of revelation in general and on the Bible in particular. The Bible represents the starting-point for Benjamin's philosophy of language, and only by allowing the Bible to evolve the fundamental linguistic facts, to communicate its spiritual being, can language be understood.

In addition to the essay on language, several early fragments on the philosophy of language refer to the Bible. One of these appears in "On Painting; or, Sign and Time" (1918):

> Absolute signs are, for example, the mark of Cain, the sign with which the houses of the Israelites were marked during the ten plagues in Egypt, and presumably the similar sign in Ali Baba and the forty thieves; one can assume, with necessary caution, that the absolute sign has a predominantly spatial and personal meaning.[24]

These absolute signs are nonlinguistic, supernatural actions; they speak for themselves as the symbolic equivalent of divine speech. Absolute signs are both subjective and objective, because they have personal and spatial meaning. They also mark crucial turning points in narrative; unlike language, the absolute sign miraculously changes the story, and by extension, history. Written around the time Benjamin was working on his study of early romantic aesthetics, this fragment brings together the familiar romantic notions of the Absolute, language, and history within a biblical framework.

If Genesis is the biblical text of language before the Fall, then prophetic lament applies after the Fall. The statement "Because it is dumb *(stumm)*, Nature mourns *(trauert)*," echoes the mourning of the land in Jeremiah 4:28 and Hosea 4:3.[25] Later, the *Trauerspiel* study analyzes this theme from the standpoint of melancholy and allegorical language. This silence and mourning follow a trajectory to the churches of Moscow (1927): "Die Kirchen sind fast verstummt":

> The city is as good as free of the chimes that on Sundays spread such deep melancholy over our cities. . . . But the glow *(Glut)* that now shines only occasionally from the altars into the snow has been well preserved in the wooden cities of booths. In their snow-covered, narrow alleyways it is quiet. One hears only the soft jargon of the Jewish clothiers in their stalls next to the junk of the paper dealer, who, enthroned in concealment behind silver chains, has drawn tinsel and cotton-wool-tufted Father Christmases across her face like an Oriental veil.[26]

With typical ambivalence and insight, Benjamin portrays Moscow as a place where religion and commerce, Christianity and Judaism, intertwine. His observations center more on Russian religious culture than on Soviet political economy. The same logic of displacement that operates early in the theory of language and late in "On the Concept of History" appears here: the glow of the churches has shifted outside, to the market stalls. Commodity culture overtakes religion, which is itself far removed from pure, divine language. Moscow's post-revolutionary churches stand nearly silent and dark, but something—a glow, a profane illumination from the religious kitsch of the paper vendor—preserves the scriptural function. This remarkable description captures the same dialectics of sacred and profane, idealism and materialism, presence and absence, that underlie the theory of language.

### "Toward the Critique of Violence" (1921)

One of Benjamin's most misunderstood attempts to practice the recovery of pure language is his 1921 attack on the foundations of jurisprudence, "Toward the Critique of Violence" (or "force"; *Gewalt* can denote either).[27] The essay appears at first to be a confused collection of reflections on law, violence, communication, Georges Sorel's theory of the general strike, and the distinction between divine and mythic violence. Like many of Benjamin's essays, "The Critique of Violence" states a set of problems and sketches their solution only inconclusively. While it may appear incomplete, I suggest that the essay self-consciously employs the rhetoric of the task in order to outline and demonstrate a novel and coherent intellectual project that requires further analysis.

The coherence of the essay emerges from the connection between violence and law. State-sanctioned violence, typically construed as a means to preserving legal ends, actually makes rather than preserves law, according to Benjamin. In this sense, violence is "not a means but a manifestation."[28] The justification of violence as a means of preserving law is thus reversed by Benjamin, who argues that violence as such never represents a rational, justified means to a just end. Benjamin also distinguishes between mythic violence and its opposite, divine violence:

> If mythical violence is lawmaking, divine violence is law-destroying; if the former sets boundaries, the latter boundlessly destroys them; if mythical violence brings at once guilt and retribution, divine power only expiates; if the former threatens, the latter strikes; if the former is bloody, the latter is lethal without spilling blood.[29]

Divine law, which *underlies* natural law and the state for Aquinas, Hobbes, and Locke, here *explodes* the law of the state; divine law is no law[30] at all but rather divine violence and hence revelation or manifestation rather than enforcement. Divine law represents the pure language of judgment and therefore has very little in common with law as it is ordinarily conceived. Unlike mythic or human law, divine law exhibits the features of pure language as mimesis, name, and revelation; as such, divine law requires no justification: it simply appears.

The concept of divine violence evokes the "judging word" of divine punishment in the essay on language. In the banishment from Eden, the judging word of God replaces the divine word of creation, causing the deterioration of language into the mere sign, chatter *(Geschwätz)*, and abstraction: "The tree of knowledge did not stand in the garden of God in order to dispense information on good and evil, but as an emblem of judgment over the questioner. This immense irony marks the mythical origin of law."[31] Divine law and divine violence precede rather than follow from an abstract system of principles.

Benjamin's example of divine violence in "Critique of Violence" is biblical: the punishment for the rebellion of Korah in Numbers 16:

> Just as in all spheres God opposes myth, mythical violence is confronted by the divine. . . . The legend of Niobe may be confronted, as an example of this violence, with God's judgment on the company of Korah. It strikes privileged Levites, strikes them without warning, without threat, and does not stop short of annihilation. But in annihilating it also expiates, and a deep connection between the lack of bloodshed and the expiatory character of this violence is unmistakable. . . . Mythical violence is bloody power over mere life for its own sake, divine violence pure power over all life for the sake of the living. The first demands sacrifice, the second accepts it.[32]

Judgment, punishment, and expiation occur at one stroke with divine violence, which precedes any abstract principle. Mythical violence, on the contrary, makes and institutionalizes laws, and is therefore reprehensible *(verwerflich)*.[33] The essay combines political and theological objectives in an unstable but critical way without attempting to reconcile them. Its conclusion represents human powerlessness in the face of divine violence, in contrast to the human empowerment of Sorel's general strike:

> Once again all the eternal forms are open to pure divine violence, which myth bastardized with law. It may manifest itself in a true war exactly as in the divine judgment on a criminal. But all mythical, lawmaking violence, which we may call executive *(schaltende)*, is pernicious. . . . Divine violence, which is the sign

and seal but never the means *(Mittel)* of sacred execution, may be called sovereign *(waltende)* violence.[34]

"The Critique of Violence" attacks the philosophy of natural law from political and theological directions without synthesizing these two approaches in the form of alternative praxis; far from representing an available solution to mythical and state-sanctioned violence, divine violence represents a critical horizon against which human violence can be understood.[35] In the terms of Benjamin's philosophy of language, however, the essay opposes mythical and legal violence because it characterizes the bourgeois language of abstraction. Numbers 16 depicts a case of divine violence in the divine word of judgment; as in the essay on language, the sacred text of the Bible evolves the fundamental linguistic facts.

The brief but forceful interpretation deliberately ignores the divine rationale for wiping out Korah and his fellow mutineers; no reason or context for the slaughter is given. The point Benjamin wishes to make is not that disobedience to God or Moses deserves severe punishment or even that things were better in ancient Israel. Rather, the violent episode in Numbers illustrates divine violence as the antipode to mythical and legal violence: "[N]either divine judgment, nor the grounds for this judgment, can be known in advance."[36] This applies even to the most legalistic of biblical injunctions: the commandment "Thou shalt not kill"

> exists not as a criterion of judgment, but as a guideline for the actions of persons or communities who have to wrestle with it in solitude and, in exceptional cases, to take on themselves the responsibility of ignoring it. Thus it was understood by Judaism, which expressly rejected the condemnation of killing in self-defense.[37]

Divine law needs no justification and forms no systematic basis for human laws. Judaism and the Hebrew Bible provide the same kind of limit case in the philosophy of law as they do in the language essay. The Bible exerts authority, but it is a negative authority that provides a standpoint for Benjamin's radical critique.

In a fragment on law from around 1919, Benjamin defines politics as "the fulfillment of unrealized human responsibility":

> it cannot mean: excused by religion, rather it must mean required by the legislation of the profane. The Mosaic laws probably do not belong to it without exception. Rather they belong to the legislation over the worldly area in the broadest sense (presumably) and have a completely special position; they determine the type and territory of *unmediated* divine action.[38]

Divine law opposes human, mythical law in the same way that pure language opposes human language. The Mosaic law of the Bible constitutes absolute, divine authority rather than mediated, human law.

## Trauerspiel, Messianism, and Modernity

The biblical model of sacred text places history after the Fall, even if this is only a metaphor.[39] Alienated from pure language and divine origins, historical time fits between creation and redemption in salvation history. Several early texts show the extent to which Benjamin related the Bible and religion to history. A 1918 fragment shows a taxonomy of world history, divine history, and natural history.[40] Another text from that period, "The Flag," links the tower of Babel to images of Christian eschatology: "The flag at the resurrection—Christ holds it: it belongs to the provisions of eschatological places. The flag over the world. Flagpole—tower. Tower into the sky (Babel)[.] Was a flagpole once built step by step (like a tower, *not* a pillar)?"[41] Like the dialectical images he imagined much later in the Arcades project, "The Flag" confronts ideas of time, symbol, and salvation in visual, provocative terms.

Messianism preoccupied Benjamin from his youth until the year of his death, when he wrote "On the Concept of History." "Trauerspiel und Tragödie" and "Die Bedeutung der Sprache in Trauerspiel und Tragödie," both from 1916, contrast history and messianism through the example of the Bible:[42]

> The time of history is endless in every way and unfulfilled in every moment. . . . This idea of fulfilled time in the Bible is the

reigning historical idea: messianic time. But in every case the idea of fulfilled historical time is not considered also as individual time. This definition, which naturally transforms the sense of "fulfillment" completely, says that tragic time differs from messianic time. Tragic time relates to the latter, as the individual fulfilled time relates to divine fulfilled time.[43]

Messianic time is fulfilled, but not in the definitive sense in which tragic time is fulfilled. These two early texts on *Trauerspiel,* which anticipate many of the themes of the 1925 book-length study, illustrate the kind of "fundamental facts" about language to which Benjamin refers in the language essay he wrote the same year (1916). The theme of messianism also appears in the 1919 dissertation on early romantic aesthetics, where Benjamin saw messianism as central to romanticism;[44] in the 1921 essay on translation; and most famously in the 1921 "Theological–Political Fragment" and the 1940 "On the Concept of History," where it takes on its most explicitly political meaning.[45]

Like divine language and divine law, Benjamin's messianism represents a limit beyond human capacities and experience. Just as language can never properly be considered a means toward an end, so "nothing historical can relate itself on its own account to anything Messianic."[46] The best one can hope to accomplish is the "weak Messianic power" described in "On the Concept of History." For the most part, Benjamin sees historical epochs as a succession of failed human efforts to recover the pure language of the past or to realize the messianic hopes for the future.

Two of the key moments in this "salvation history" are the German baroque and the Reformation, on which Benjamin concentrates in the *Trauerspiel* study:

Whereas in the decades of the Counter-Reformation Catholicism had penetrated secular life with all the power of its discipline, the relationship of Lutheranism to the everyday had always been antinomic. The rigorous morality of its teaching in respect of civic conduct stood in sharp contrast to its renunciation of "good works." By denying the latter any special miraculous spiritual effect, making the soul dependent on grace through faith, and making the secular-political sphere a testing ground for a life which was only indirectly religious, being intended for the demonstration of civic virtues, it did, it is true, instil into the people a strict sense of obedience to duty, but in its great men it produced melancholy.[47]

The antinomies of Lutheranism are the antinomies of allegory and the Bible: the clash between meaningful and meaningless, sacred and secular, ideal and real.

The melancholy book culture of the baroque appealed to Benjamin's temperament: "The Renaissance explores the universe; the baroque explores libraries. Its meditations are devoted to books."[48] More importantly, it displayed the critical potential of the scriptural function. Max Pensky observes:

> In the baroque, the relation between the melancholy subject and its a priori objects comes into a particularly pregnant state, insofar as the specific historical conditions of physical and spiritual devastation approach the true state of affairs in human history. Such rare moments—for example, the *Trauerspiel,* the allegory of Baudelaire, the motions of Proustian memory— radiate messianic energy like beacons, because they promise to reveal themselves as sites where critical work can find images in which the whole of historical time, of an epoch, or of an era is compressed.[49]

Paradoxically, it is because of their awkward failure to reinstate pure language that these periods draw Benjamin's attention. The further one gets from pure language, the easier it is to approach critically.

Benjamin compares the Renaissance and Reformation to modernity in *One-Way Street (Einbahnstrasse):*

> Just as this time is the antithesis of the Renaissance in general, it contrasts in particular to the situation in which the art of

printing was discovered. For whether by coincidence or not, its appearance in Germany came at a time when the book in the most eminent sense of the word, the book of books, had through Luther's translation become the people's property *(Volksgut)*. Now everything indicates that the book in this traditional form is nearing its end. . . .Writing *(Die Schrift)*, which had found a refuge in printed books where it could lead an autonomous existence, is pitilessly dragged out onto the street by advertisements and subjected to the brutal heteronomies of economic chaos.[50]

Because of context and because *die Schrift* also means "scripture," the refuge for writing is also the refuge for the Bible.

In different ways, the *Trauerspiel* study and *Einbahnstrasse* develop the conception of sacred text as an archive of pure language; sacred texts attest to the possibility of a pure language of naming and to its loss. The antinomies of allegory are also the antinomies of sacred texts, which negotiate the contradiction between self-expression and ordinary meaning, "sacred standing and profane comprehensibility." As writing, sacred texts are both the most fallible, fallen form of communication, as opposed to the pure language of spoken names, and at the same time the most conducive to critical recovery of pure language. Pure language itself is blocked from contemporary understanding, and efforts to recover it must therefore proceed through the channels of the post-Lapsarian language of judgment, mere signs, and abstraction. Access to pure language remains always indirect and incomplete; Benjamin's philosophical criticism of texts charts this course.

*One-Way Street* advances the philosophical task of recovering pure language through experimental writing. As a highly self-conscious book about books, it follows the stylistic critical tradition of Novalis.[51] At the same time, *One-Way Street* pursues the biblical and textual interests of the essays on language and translation: "On the tree of the sacred text," commentary and translation are "eternally rustling leaves *(Blätter)*," while on the profane commentary and translation are "seasonally-falling fruits."[52]

## *"Karl Kraus"* (1931)

Like Kafka and Rosenzweig, Karl Kraus offered Benjamin a model of the Jewish intellectual who creatively engages the scriptural function. Like Baudelaire, Kraus also represented a devilish figure in the hell of modern culture: "Only Baudelaire hated as Kraus did the satiety of healthy common sense, and the compromise that intellectuals made with it in order to find shelter in journalism."[53] For the relatively obscure Benjamin, Kraus also represented the success of writing as political and cultural practice. The essay shows remarkable continuity with the early philosophy of language and law, and it also anticipates many themes of the artwork essay, the Arcades project, and "On the Idea of History." If the numerous manuscripts are any indication, "Karl Kraus" is also one of Benjamin's most heavily drafted and revised writings.[54]

Kraus is "the destructive character" who "knows only one watchword: make room; only one activity: clearing away."[55] But he is also the angel of "old engravings," Klee's *Angelus Novus*, and "On the Concept of History," bringing the urgent message of "real humanism" against the "empty phrase": "He stands on the threshold of the Last Judgment.... If he ever turns his back on creation, if he breaks out in lamentation, it is only to file a complaint at the Last Judgment."[56]

The "liberation of language" is Kraus's primary concern; for Benjamin he represents the best opponent of the same linguistic "prattle" *(Geschwätz)* Benjamin decries in the essay on language.[57] Kraus's attack on journalism recalls Benjamin's lament that newspapers subject writing *(die Schrift)* to commodification. At the other extreme are the poetic mystifications of Stefan George, which Benjamin characterizes as a kind of linguistic idolatry:

> To the cosmic rising and falling that for George "deifies the body and embodies the divine," language is only the Jacob's ladder with its ten thousand word-rungs. Kraus's language, by contrast, has done away with all hieratic moments.... It is

the theater of a sanctification of the name—with this Jewish certainty it sets itself against the theurgy of the "word–body."[58]

While Kraus was criticized during his lifetime as "a shining example of Jewish self-hatred," Benjamin clearly saw his Jewishness as a positive feature of his recovery of language in the terms set out in the essays on language and violence:

> It has been said of Kraus that he has to "suppress the Jewishness in himself," even that he "travels the road from Jewishness to freedom"; nothing better refutes this than the fact that, for him, too, justice and language remain founded in each other. To worship the image of divine justice in language—even in the German language—that is the genuinely Jewish somersault by which he tries to break the spell of the demon.[59]

Though demonic, Kraus's Judaism is authentic and essential to his critical work; it represents a forceful version of the "cultural Zionism" Benjamin selected for himself in 1912.[60] Kraus's Jewish praxis overlaps with Benjamin's: the retrieval of divine language and law through strategies of silence, quotation, satire, and "biblical pathos."[61] Benjamin compares him to an ethereal figure from the Talmud raising his voice to God.[62]

Kafka, that other Jewish writer who preoccupied Benjamin in the 1930s, has none of the destructive grandiosity of Kraus; rather, he embodies the characteristics of "the storyteller." But Kafka shares Kraus's concern for biblical language and law. Like the bumbling Abraham of Kafka's parable, who appears "with the promptness of a waiter," Kafka fails "in his grandiose attempt to convert poetry into doctrine," but by ordering the destruction of his writings, Benjamin observes, "No other writer has obeyed the commandment 'Thou shalt not make unto thee a graven image' so faithfully."[63]

Like translation, Kraus's technique of quotation evokes the pure, biblical language of naming:

> To quote a word is to call it by its name. . . . In quotation the two realms—of origin and destruction—justify themselves

before language. And conversely, only where they inter-penetrate—in quotation—is language consummated. In it is mirrored the angelic tongue in which all words, startled from the idyllic context of meaning, have become mottoes in the book of Creation.[64]

Searching for urgent voices of critique, Benjamin identifies Kraus as a demonic, angelic, and even messianic model of the recovery of language he sought to undertake. Lashing out at the empty commercialism of popular journalism and the grandiosity of the George Circle, Kraus embodies the Jewish critical spirit that understands the degraded condition of language. Kraus engaged the biblical genres of Genesis, lament, and apocalypse and their corresponding epochs.

More for its sacred status *(Geltung)* than its contents, Benjamin approaches the Bible as an archive of pure language. Biblical narratives of origin, loss, judgment, and messianic promise run through Benjamin's biblical citations. Even the *Passagen-Werk*, which deals more with cultural history than texts, is replete with biblical imagery, although it is often viewed through the lens of an allegorist. In Benjamin's comments on Baudelaire's poem "Abel et Caïn," for instance, Cain appears as the founder of a proletarian race.[65] The following chapter examines how Benjamin's theory of history developed from the biblical project of recovering pure language.

## NOTES

1. *GS* 2: 891; the passage refers to Matthew 5.
2. See the scene in *Berliner Chronik* where he can't find the synagogue, *GS* 6: 512. See also the 1940 (May 7) letter to Adorno where Benjamin notes Marcel Proust's insight into the "precarious structure," Jewish assimilation in France, especially after the Dreyfus campaign, *Briefe* 2: 853.
3. See the 1912 and 1913 letters to Ludwig Strauss on the subjects of Zionism and Judaism, *GS* 2: 835–44.
4. McCole, *Walter Benjamin and the Antinomies of Tradition*, 66–67.
5. See chapters 2 and 3.
6. Letter to Scholem, 3/30/18, *Briefe*, 1:181.

7. An excellent study of these themes, though it makes little mention of the Bible, is Irving Wohlfarth, "On Some Jewish Motifs in Benjamin," in *Problems of Modernity,* ed. Andrew Benjamin (Chicago: University of Chicago Press, 1989), 157–213.

8. For example, he compares Stefan George to a prophet in a letter to Scholem (June 16, 1933, *Briefe* 2: 578) and Hugo von Hofmannsthal to Christ in a letter to Adorno (May 7, 1940, *Briefe* 2: 852).

9. From John 1:1, *GS* 4: 18.

10. Rosenzweig, *The Star of Redemption,* 340.

11. See "Theses," in *Illuminations,* 254, and "Theologisch-Politisches Fragment," *GS* 2: 203–4.

12. See the letter in which Benjamin ascribes anti-Semitism to the Christian reading of the Old Testament and history:

> In this regard, one motive . . . that must be considered is the extremely spurious and distorted method, now become historical, in which an acknowledgment of the coming Christian centuries and peoples was imposed upon the Old Testament by the oldest Christian churches and congregations. This was, of course, originally done in the hope of wresting the Old Testament from the Jews, and without an awareness of historical consequences, since people lived in anticipation of the imminent end. (Letter to Scholem 10/22/17, *Briefe* 1:153, trans. in *The Correspondence of Walter Benjamin,* trans. Manfred and Evelyn Jacobson [Chicago: University of Chicago Press, 1994], 99–100)

13. Nägele, *Theater, Theory, Speculation,* 82–83.

14. "On Language," in *Reflections,* 323.

15. Ibid.

16. Ibid., 330; "Über Sprache," *GS* 2: 155.

17. "On Language," in *Reflections,* 323; "Über Sprache," *GS* 2: 142.

18. "On Language," in *Reflections,* 327.

19. Ibid.

20. Ibid.

21. "Über Sprache," 153. See also the fragment on word, name, object, and sign in *GS* 6: 11–14, where the *blosse Zeichen* occupies a tertiary and indirect position among linguistic elements.

22. "On Language," in *Reflections,* 327–28; see also "Critique of Violence."

23. "On Language," in *Reflections,* 329–30.

24. *GS* 2:604.

25. *GS* 1: 155.

26. *Reflections,* 127–28, *GS* 4:344.

27. *Reflections,* 277–300, *GS* 2: 179–203.

28. "Critique of Violence," 294.

29. Ibid., 297. Cf. the Prologue to the *Trauerspiel* study: "A major work will either establish the genre or abolish it; and the perfect work will do both," 44.

30. "Critique of Violence," 298.

31. Ibid.

32. Ibid., 297.

33. *GS* 2: 203.

34. "Critique of Violence," 300; *GS* 2: 203.

35. This interpretation differs markedly from that of Jacques Derrida, who suggests that the essay might leave open the "temptation to think the holocaust as an uninterpretable manifestation of divine violence," "Force of Law: The 'Mystical Foundation of Authority,'" trans. Mary Quaintance, *Cardozo Law Review* 11 (1990): 1044. Perhaps because the text is already so unstable, Derrida's attempt to read deconstructively, against the grain of the essay, leads to a reductionistic interpretation that implicates it in fascist modes of thought by invoking Carl Schmitt and Heidegger. But like pure language, divine violence is inaccessible, and the essay quite clearly sets forth a number of incompatible models of *Gewalt*, including the general strike, natural law, and divine law, without resolving them. The provisional title of the essay, "Zur Kritik der Gewalt," employs the rhetoric of the task to show all the antinomies and competing discourses that a critique of force would have to reconcile.

36. *Reflections*, 298.

37. Ibid.

38. *GS* 6: 99.

39. See chapter 5.

40. *GS* 6: 92–93.

41. *GS* 6: 94–95.

42. *GS* 2: 133, 197.

43. "Trauerspiel und Tragödie," *GS* 2: 134.

44. See *Briefe* 1: 134–39 and *GS* 1: 12.

45. As the "Fragment" shows, religion and politics are linked much earlier than Benjamin's so-called Marxist period. See also the 1921 "Capitalism as Religion," *GS* 6: 100–103.

46. "Theologico-Political Fragment," *Reflections*, 312.

47. *Origin*, 138.

48. *Origin*, 140.

49. Max Pensky, *Melancholy Dialectics* (Amherst: University of Massachusetts Press, 1993), 94.

50. *Reflections*, 77, with my changes; *GS* 4:102.

51. See Novalis's aphorisms on books in *German Romantic Criticism*, A. Leslie Willson, ed., trans. Alexander Gelley (New York: Continuum, 1982), 66–67.

52. *One-Way Street*, in *Reflections*, 68.

53. *Reflections*, 258; *GS* 2: 345–54. On the image of modernity as hell, see *GS* 5:1010–11. On Baudelaire, see *GS* 1:523–24.

54. See the editorial materials in *GS* 2: 1078–1130.

55. *Reflections*, 301.

56. Ibid., 254, 272.

57. *Reflections*, 242.

58. Ibid., 265.

59. *Reflections*, 254; Theodor Lessing, *Der jüdische Selbsthass* (Berlin: Jüdischer Verlag, 1930), 43, cited in Introduction to *Half-Truths and One-and-a-Half Truths:*

*Karl Kraus, Selected Aphorisms,* trans. Harry Zohn (Chicago: University of Chicago Press, 1990), 7.

60. Kraus himself criticized political Zionism in the 1898 *Eine Krone für Zion;* cited in Kraus, 6.

61. *GS* 2:336, *Reflections,* 242–43, 268.

62. *Reflections,* 273.

63. *Illuminations,* 129.

64. *Reflections,* 268–69.

65. *GS* 1: 523.

# CHAPTER 6

# The Scriptural Function of Contemporary Culture

History is a shock between tradition and political organization.[1]

$B$enjamin's concept of sacred text as the archive of pure language develops from his linguistic theory. From the hermeneutical perspective of modernity, the sacred text of the Bible constitutes the foundation of linguistic theory. But as an *archive* of pure language, the sacred text is by definition always a late phenomenon; the sacred requires and opposes the profane. Pure language deteriorates into abstract language, the language of judgment, and the mere sign. As archive, the sacred text preserves pure language but also narrates its loss, just as language functions as an archive of the mimetic faculty. Because it relies on historical categories, the linguistic theory of sacred text calls for a theory of history. Benjamin's historiographic writings provide a methodological and substantive basis for the linguistic theory of sacred texts. The theory of history advanced in the early fragments and essays, in "On the Concept of History," and in the *Passagen-Werk* reflects the interplay of traditional and modern, sacred and profane, found in the theory of language.

Benjamin's conception of modernity has its roots in the theory of allegory. Just as the *Trauerspiel* allegorizes Christian stories in the baroque period, so Baudelaire allegorizes Christianity for modern culture. The theory of language thus precedes the theory of history; unlike nineteenth-century philosophers such as Humboldt, Benjamin develops a linguistic theory of history rather than a historical theory of language.[2] The dualisms of pure and historical language, and sacred and profane texts, which Benjamin revises in dialectical terms, imply a theory of history and contemporary culture, and the objective of the work on Baudelaire and the Paris Arcades was to provide such a theory. Modernity for Benjamin is linked to sacred texts, the archival receptacles of pure language in contemporary times. On the one hand, modernity stands for everything novel and shocking; on the other, it simply restates familiar categories in new terms: "Definition of the 'modern' as the new in relationship to what has always already been."[3] In opposition to the typically modern celebration of progress, Benjamin's notion of modernity reiterates tradition. History is accordingly defined in such synchronic terms as shock, dialectics at a standstill, and *Jetztzeit*, which focus on the momentary and illuminating suspension of time.

German historiography around the turn of the century was deeply concerned with the problems of modernity and historicism. Philosophers and historians, including Max Weber, Wilhelm Dilthey, and Leopold von Ranke, addressed questions about the status of historical understanding as well as the status of the modern period. Was history a scientific discipline? Could historical studies accurately and thoroughly describe historical phenomena? By what means? Was the modern period a secular age? In his Arcades project, "On the Concept of History," and "The Storyteller," Benjamin entered these debates forcefully and self-consciously. Beginning with a critique of historicism and the ideology of progress, Benjamin's notions of history and modernity advance his general philosophical program by emphasizing the dependence of ostensibly secular culture on theological categories.

For Buber and Rosenzweig, modernity takes form in the secularized Enlightenment humanism alienated from its sacred origins. Both thinkers call for the personal recovery of spiritual experience through a return to the Bible. For Benjamin, on the other hand, modernity represents a complete transformation of experience by new urban and technological phenomena. Instead of describing these changes in terms of profane secularization, he links them to a subtle view of the sacred-secular opposition. Like the allegory of the German *Trauerspiel,* modern experience preserves religious and sacred phenomena through new expressions.[4] Modernity paradoxically affirms the persistence of sacred phenomena that lie beyond the reach of contemporary experience.[5]

Benjamin's theory of history has two main dimensions: compositional and epistemological. To support the philosophical restoration of pure language, the writings on history employ innovative compositional techniques such as montage, aphorisms, quotation, and the rhetoric of the task. The notion of modernity emerges from a linguistic theory of history rather than from a historical theory of language. In this way, sacred text, as an archive of pure language, remains as central to Benjamin's late work as it is to the early work. These compositional techniques form the basis of an epistemological strategy of understanding history and experience that has philosophical, religious, aesthetic, and political dimensions.

Stéphane Mosès has suggested that Benjamin's theory of history has three successive stages: theological, aesthetic, and political.[6] While these modes of discourse appear in Benjamin's different writings on history, this view implies drastic shifts in Benjamin's thought. In my view, the different statements on history reflect different applications of a consistent linguistic and theological theory of history. This theory elaborates the basic post-Lapsarian model of language and promotes the restoration of pure language through compositional and epistemological means; the paradigm for this activity is the biblical notion of sacred text, the archive of pure language.[7] Even in the historical materialism of "On the Concept of History" and the Arcades project, sacred text plays this central role with respect to critical understanding and the recovery of pure language. The following analysis sketches Benjamin's philosophy of history as it relates to the concepts of modernity and sacred text, first in the essays on religion, surrealism, mechanically reproducible art, storytelling, and Kafka, and secondly, in the "On the Concept of History" and the *Passagen-Werk*.

## Benjamin's Early Philosophy of History

Benjamin's theory of history and modernity has its antecedents in the *Trauerspiel* study and *Einbahnstrasse*. The melancholy allegory of the *Trauerspiel* occupies a present constructed on the fragments of the past, an age during which the recovery of revelation is necessary but impossible. The experimental compositional technique of *Einbahnstrasse* represents the novelty of modern culture through juxtaposition, irony, and reversals of conventional notions of writing, the sacred, and art. The problem of history also appears in the earlier essays on language, where the category of sacred text is identified as the primary archive of pure language after the Fall. But it is not until the later work on Baudelaire, the Arcades project, and "On the Concept of History" that the conception of history becomes more fully theorized. Only through a careful analysis of the modern situation could the implications of the loss of pure language be understood.

The theory of history and modernity draws not only from the study of texts but also from the materialist study of objects and images as texts. The aim of Benjamin's history is to create brief, shocklike insights that have both political and messianic potential. In modern culture, the fundamental structure of experience changes while its allegorical structure remains unchanging. The reading of allegorical texts in the *Trauerspiel* becomes the study of Baudelaire's dialectical image, a compressed expression of cultural contradictions that brings thought to a halt: "If it can be said that for Baudelaire modern life is the foundation of the dialectical images then included therein is the fact that Baudelaire confronted modern life in a way comparable to that in which the 17th century confronted antiquity."[8] Benjamin's notions of modernity and history reflect the loss of pure language, in contrast to such notions as progress and universal history:

> (The idea of a universal history hinges on the idea of a universal language. As long as the latter was grounded either in theology, as in the Middle Ages, or in logic, most recently by Leibniz, universal history was not unthinkable. As practised since the nineteenth century, however, universal history can never be anything but a kind of esperanto.) . . . It can have no objective basis until the confusion that stems from the tower of Babel has been settled.[9]

Irving Wohlfarth notes, "In grounding a universal history on a universal language, Benjamin's very last speculations revert to the philosophy of language set forth in his early essays."[10] If the goal of Benjamin's early philosophy is to recover lost pure language, then the epistemological categories and compositional techniques of Benjamin's theory of history are designed to ground and fulfill that task. The emergence of the theory of history can be seen in the essays on religion, aesthetics, and narrative, analyses of which follow.

## *"Dialogue on the Religiosity of the Present" (1912)*

Benjamin's earliest writings on religion reflect the idealistic youth movement of which he was a member until 1915, when he became disillusioned with its leaders' support for the war.[11] In the spirit of Gustav Wyneken, the 1912 "Dialog Über die Religiosität der Gegenwart" considers the position of religion in contemporary culture through a debate between a first-person speaker and "the friend."[12] The speaker characterizes true religion as a "metaphysical seriousness" that has lost its dominance, and the friend dismisses religion as "laziness."[13] Against the friend's various definitions of religion as superstition, skepticism, and individualism, the speaker elaborates a notion of new religion of contemporary culture that "gives a new ground and a new nobility to daily life and to convention."[14] Among the prophets of this "new religious consciousness" are Ibsen, Tolstoy, Nietzsche, and Strindberg.[15]

The dialogue reaches the subject of religion through aesthetics. In reference to *l'art pour l'art*, the "I" character notes: "We are irreligious, because we no longer notice that which is persistent. Do you notice how they pull out the end-in-itself, this last sanctification of a goal? How everything individual, which doesn't become clear and honest, becomes an 'end-in-itself.'"[16] The speaker sketches an alternative, literary notion of modern religion in the tradition of Kantian philosophy and romanticism centered on the conflict between self and society: "I believe the works that touch us most fiercely in the first encounter, that most of all Ibsen and naturalism bear this new religious consciousness"; this new religion "gives daily life a new ground and a new nobility."[17] Contemporary religion gains relevance from the problem of knowledge in and about the contemporary period:

If knowledge itself is not problematic, a religion, which begins with urgencies, will not have to bother itself with knowledge. And there has hardly been a time in which knowledge was contested in a naturally problematic way. Historical misunderstandings have brought it only so far. And this most modern problem, about which pages are full, arises because they don't ask themselves from the ground up about the religion of the time; rather they ask whether one of the historical religions could still find a lodging in it and whether they cut off their arms and bones and the head as well.[18]

The dialogue presents a theory of religion as a declining but not obsolete phenomenon; despite the process of secularization, religion can be revived and transformed through a new religious consciousness that restores the metaphysical seriousness and awareness of the persistent in the face of modern everyday life. Far from being superseded by modern culture, religion regains vitality through self-transformation and the recognition of daily life. At the same time, this new religion arises principally from literature and philosophy, thus blurring the traditional distinction between religious and secular, sacred and profane.

For Benjamin, this modern literary conception of religion was bound to his own Jewish identity. In a letter to Ludwig Strauss from the same series in which he articulated the idea of "cultural Zionism," Benjamin comments on the "Dialogue" as part of a Jewish literary movement:

Even the best West-European Jews are no longer free as Jews. They could join the Jewish movement only in the sense that your letter suggests. For they are linked to the literary movement. . . .Through being or will, the Jews today, as far as they are scientific, literary and commercial leaders, are bound to internationalism. . . .Their [the Jewish literati] most serious mission is to gain *Geist* for the times out of art which they cannot themselves make. . . .Heinrich Mann asks in Sombart's "Judentaufen": Where would *Geist*, love, and art be among us without the Jews? It certainly can't be said that political Zionism

works against such Jewish cultural work—nevertheless, it lies
removed and unconnected from them in practice.[19]

Western-European Jews lead the international cultivation of *Geist*
as it appears in literature.

Two later essays, "Die religiöse Stellung der neuen Jugend" (1914)
and "Das Leben der Studenten" (1915), begin to part ways with
the political standpoint of Wyneken's youth movement, but they
still identify youth with religion: "Youth, which declares itself for
itself, *means* religion, which does not yet exist."[20] The youth must
make choices and struggle in order to bring about this religion and
an accompanying sense of the sacred.[21] After completing one version
of "The Life of Students," Benjamin added a cautionary statement
against realizing idealist goals by pragmatic means:

> To form the immanent state of perfection into one utterly abso-
> lute, to make it visible and dominant in the present is the
> historical task *(Aufgabe)*. But this state of things is not to be
> circumscribed by a pragmatic depiction of particulars (institu-
> tions, customs, and so on); on the contrary, it eludes such
> portrayal. It can be caught hold of only in its metaphysical
> structure, as in the messianic realm or the French idea of
> revolution.[22]

Equally reluctant to give up idealism or the youth movement as
its main vehicle, Benjamin adopts the rhetoric of the task and
messianism as ways of affirming and deferring idealist goals.

### Art and Aura: Surrealism and "The Work of Art in the Age of Its Technical Reproducibility"

The essays on surrealism (1929) and "The Work of Art in the Age
of Its Technical Reproducibility" (1936/1939) attach a mixture of
the sacred and the profane, as well as optimism and pessimism,
to modern aesthetic phenomena.[23] Surrealist art and technically
reproduced art such as film have both progressive and regressive
potential with respect to the recovery of pure language and the
realization of political ends. Surrealism is a dialectical artistic and

political movement in which "language takes precedence."[24] Surrealism strives toward "profane illumination," which Benjamin defines as "a materialistic, anthropological inspiration, to which hashish, opium, or whatever else can give an introductory lesson."[25] Nevertheless, surrealism contains "pernicious romantic prejudices," such as the uncritical obsession with intoxication and the occult:

> Any serious exploration of occult, surrealistic, phantasmagoric gifts and phenomena presupposes a dialectical intertwinement to which a romantic turn of mind is impervious. For histrionic or fanatical stress on the mysterious side of the mysterious takes us no further; we penetrate the mystery only to the degree that we recognize it in the everyday world, by virtue of a dialectical optic that perceives the everyday as impenetrable, the impenetrable as everyday. The most passionate investigation of telepathic phenomena, for example, will not teach us half as much about reading (which is an eminently telepathic process), as the profane illumination of reading about telepathic phenomena. . . . The reader, the thinker, the loiterer, the *flâneur,* are types of illuminati just as much as the opium eater, the dreamer, the ecstatic. And more profane.[26]

The reading and writing of texts yields greater illumination than dabbling in the occult. Like the romantics, the surrealists belong to the tradition of the scriptural function, applying new methods of writing and thought to recognizing the "impenetrable." But Benjamin accepts neither romanticism nor surrealism uncritically; profane illumination does not recover pure language any more than allegory or romantic poetry.

Like the essay on surrealism, "The Work of Art in the Age of Its Technical Reproducibility" welcomes modern aesthetic phenomena with a mixture of optimism and pessimism. Surprisingly, many interpreters since Adorno have characterized the essay as an undialectical or simplistic Marxist appropriation of technically reproducible art, a view that simply overlooks statements to the contrary within the essay.[27] The discussion of film, for instance, illustrates the two-edged tendency of modern art. On the one hand, the reproducibility of film potentially "emancipates the work of art from its parasitical dependence on ritual" through the destruction of aura that accompanies reproducible art.[28] On the other hand, "The film responds to the shriveling of the aura with an artificial buildup of the 'personality' outside the studio. The cult of the movie star, fostered by the money of the film industry, preserves not the unique aura of the person but the 'spell of the personality,' the phony spell of a commodity."[29]

Given this dark prognosis, it becomes difficult to take Benjamin's more optimistic-sounding statements literally. The claim that "The reactionary attitude toward a Picasso painting changes into the progressive reaction toward a Chaplin movie" bespeaks a sardonic tone rather than starry-eyed optimism about the new art form.[30] The loss of aura in the technically reproducible work of art may contain revolutionary potential, but in fact capitalism and fascism both exploit the new art forms (especially film) in reactionary ways that seek to preserve aura.[31] In capitalism and fascism, aura simply reappears in the technologically reproducible artwork; in the case of revolutionary art, aura is replaced by a dissolution of boundaries between author and audience, mass reception, shock, and distraction *(Zerstreuung)*, all of which contribute to a positive revolutionary consciousness: "Instead of being based on ritual, it begins to be based on another practice—politics."[32] Nevertheless, the new art forms yield new kinds of perception and experience that are analogous transformations of the experience of auratic art.[33]

The loss of aura, which is "the unique phenomenon of a distance, however close it may be," means the end of the cult-value of art, but it creates new kinds of perception—such as shock and distraction—that have progressive potential.[34] Language, too, can exhibit aura; Benjamin cites Karl Kraus's definition in "Karl Kraus" and "On Some Motifs in Baudelaire": "The closer the look one takes at a word, the greater the distance from which it looks back."[35] His own experience of aura appears most vividly in his writings on hashish, where he distinguishes authentic aura, which appears in all things, from theosophy and the spirituality of "vulgar mystical books."[36] Benjamin also finds the notion of aura in Novalis and the *mémoire involontaire* of Proust.[37] Modern art and literature do not destroy aura so much as they transform it; new art forms and experiences inherit biblical tradition and have the potential to evoke it effectively.

## Narrative and History:
### Leskov and Kafka

The counterpart to the loss of aura in visual art is the loss of storytelling in literature. Benjamin's essay "The Storyteller" (1936) connects the emerging conception of modern history to narrative through the works of Nikolai Leskov.[38] The essay asserts that in modern times, storytelling is declining because "experience has fallen in value."[39] The essay sketches a gradual progression from story to information: "The earliest symptom of a process whose end is the decline of storytelling is the rise of the novel at the beginning of modern times. What distinguishes the novel from the story (and from the epic in the narrower sense) is its essential dependence on the book."[40] The transition from storytelling to information parallels the deterioration of pure language into mere signs. Storytelling thus functions like sacred texts as an archive of pure language, by representing genuine "mouth to mouth" experience as opposed to information, which has only passing interest.[41] The process of deterioration, variously explained in the essay by World War I, the rise of the novel, newspapers, and the decline of medieval chronicles, is qualified by a disclaimer:

> This, however, is a process that has been going on for a long time. And nothing would be more fatuous than to want to see in it merely a "symptom of decay," let alone a "modern" symptom. It is, rather, only a concomitant symptom of the secular productive forces of history, a concomitant that has quite gradually removed narrative from the realm of living speech and at the same time is making it possible to see a new beauty in what is vanishing.[42]

The gradual decline of storytelling must not be understood simplistically as a sudden modernization or secularization. Like the exchange of aura for shock in the artwork essay, a "new beauty" appears in the decline of storytelling. The sacred–profane distinction appears in a nonlinear fashion that recalls the "sacred text" passage from *Einbahnstrasse:*

> In the storyteller the chronicler is preserved in changed form, secularized, as it were. Leskov is among those whose work displays this with particular clarity. Both the chronicler with his sacred historical orientation and the storyteller with his profane outlook are so represented in his works that in a number of his stories it can hardly be decided whether the web in which they appear is the golden fabric of a religious view of the course of things, or the multicolored fabric of a worldly view.[43]

In storytelling, the sacred and profane are indistinguishable. Whatever terms they use, however,

> all great storytellers have in common the freedom with which they move up and down the rungs of their experience as on a ladder. A ladder extending downward to the interior of the earth and disappearing into the clouds is the image for a collective experience to which even the deepest shock of every individual experience, death, constitutes no impediment or barrier.[44]

The ladder of experience, a symbol of the power and versatility of storytelling, clearly alludes to Jacob's dream in Genesis 28. Storytelling has mystical value regardless of the terms attached to it; sacred and profane are paradoxically reversed in storytelling, so that "The lower Leskov descends on the scale of created things the more obviously does his way of viewing things approach the mystical."[45]

Nothing marks the passage of time, a requirement of storytelling, more vividly than death. The source of the storyteller's authority thus lies in death, and the modern tendency to deny death accompanies the decline of storytelling.[46] The storyteller himself is a sage who tells his own life and becomes coextensive with his story, "who could let the wick of his life be consumed completely by the gentle flame of his story."[47] Like Moses and the *torah* at the end of Deuteronomy, the storyteller and the story become essentially intertwined.[48] Storytelling belongs to the biblical tradition of sacred text, as a threatened discourse that moves freely up and down the biblical ladder of experience.

Benjamin saw Kafka's narratives as the fullest contemporary expression of the storyteller's art, exhibiting the dynamics of ancient and modern, sacred and profane: "Kafka's work is an ellipse with foci that are far apart and are determined on the one hand by mystical experience (which is above all the experience of tradition) and on the other by the experience of the modern citydweller."[49] According to Benjamin, Kafka achieves this double-focus by means of a narrative art that defies easy paraphrase or explanation:

> Kafka's writings are by their nature parables. But that is their misery and their beauty, that they had to become *more* than parables. They do not modestly lie at the feet of doctrine, as aggadah lies at the feet of halakhah. When they have crouched down, they unexpectedly raise a mighty paw against it.[50]

Kafka's stories achieve autonomy from religious doctrine and even threaten to overwhelm it; in fact, they narrate a crisis in doctrine (see the reference to Torah, below). One means of achieving this effect is the deferral of the future through the time taken up by the *activity* of narrating. Telling stories halts the flow of time: "In the stories which Kafka left us, narrative art regains the significance it had in the mouth of Scheherazade: to postpone the future."[51] Progress, a term Benjamin consistently derogates, is threatened by Kafka's tradition-bound and yet modern narratives. Like the Angelus Novus of "On the Concept of History," Kafka's narratives oppose the onslaught of progress, perhaps by means of the "weak messianic power" he attributes to modern individuals.[52]

The category of sacred text is central to Benjamin's work on Kafka. Kafka's writing contains, in his view, revelatory and messianic components: "That I do not deny the component of revelation in Kafka's work already follows from my appreciation—by declaring his work to be 'distorted' *(entstellt)*—of its messianic aspect."[53] The letter continues:

> For the work of the Torah—if we abide by Kafka's account—has been thwarted *(vereitelt)*. It is in this context that the problem of

> the Scripture *(Schrift)* poses itself. Whether the pupils have lost
> it or whether they are unable to decipher *(enträtseln)* it comes
> down to the same thing, because, without the key that belongs
> to it, the Scripture is not Scripture, but life. Life as it is lived
> in the village at the foot of the hill on which the castle is built.
> It is in the attempt to metamorphose life into Scripture that I
> perceive the meaning of "reversal" *(Umkehr)*, which so many
> of Kafka's parables endeavor to bring about.[54]

In Kafka as in Deuteronomy 32, Torah becomes life. But ironically,
Kafka's Torah becomes life only when it is thwarted. This reversal
intensifies the dialectical balance in sacred texts of system *(Komplex)*
and comprehensibility outlined in the *Trauerspiel* study: in the
world of Kafka's fiction, the thwarted sacred text becomes life while
life becomes sacred text.

If the sacred text of the Bible is an archive of pure language,
then Kafka's parables are an archive of the sacred text; like Benjamin's own writings, they perform the scriptural function partly
through innovative compositional means. The writings of Kafka
and Leskov are, in a sense, contemporary sacred texts that counteract empty history and the naive optimism of progress by pointing
back to the sacred text of the Bible. By referring to the identification
of *torah* and life in Deuteronomy 32, Benjamin portrays the contemporary world as being doubly alienated—not only from pure
language but also from the archive of pure language: the Bible.
Benjamin addresses modern experience and the thwarted sacred
text by focusing critical attention on the narratives of Leskov and
Kafka, which in turn point to the sacred text of the Bible.

## History against Progress: "On the Concept of History" and the Passagen-Werk

Like narrative, Benjamin sees history as an exercise of memory
that postpones the future and blurs the boundaries between text and
life, sacred and profane. His philosophy of history simultaneously
rejects myth and affirms the sacred. The two modern myths that
Benjamin opposes are the myth of progress and the myth of secu-

larization: "Overcoming the concept of 'progress' and the concept of 'period of decline' are two sides of one and the same thing."[55] Simplistic theories of history as progress or decline are contrasted to the religious view of history.[56] The decline of storytelling and the loss of aura in works of art do not represent abrupt or complete historical processes; they are better understood as gradual dialectical transformations.

The philosophy of history in "On the Concept of History" and the Arcades project has epistemological and compositional dimensions. The epistemological dimension can be summarized by the terms "dialectical image" and "dialectics at a standstill."[57] The dialectical image is the "caesura in the movement of thought" found "wherever the tension between dialectical oppositions is greatest."[58] In order to combat the continuum of historical progress, the dialectical image fixes attention on the contradictions of history without resolving them in a Hegelian *Aufhebung;* Benjamin describes this critical illumination as dialectics at a standstill.

The notion of history as dialectical image or dialectics at a standstill redefines history from evolutionary progress to a synchronic position of the image and object:

> If the historical object is to be blasted out of the continuum of the historical process, it is because the monadological structure of the object demands it.... The historical object, by virtue of its monadological structure, discovers within itself its own forehistory and after-history. (Thus, for example, the forehistory of Baudelaire, according to current scholarship, lies in allegory, while his after-history is found in the Jugendstil.)[59]

"Dialectics at a Standstill" constitutes an historiographic counterpart to the recovery of pure language through sacred texts. Benjamin's philosophy of history identifies modern allegories (e.g., Baudelaire, the surrealists, and even artifacts) in order to recover their hidden theological content: "My thinking relates to theology the way a blotter does to ink."[60] Like pure language and sacred texts, Benjamin's thought is so thoroughly soaked with the sacred that the particular content of the sacred has been lost. History always remains theological, though not visibly so.

In fact, theology constitutes the methodological basis for Benjamin's notion of history: "Keep reminding oneself that the commentary on reality (since here it is a question of commentary, a construing of detail) calls for a method completely different from that required for a text. In the one case theology is the basic science, in the other philology."[61] As commentaries, Benjamin's studies of architecture and commodity culture in the *Passagen-Werk* depend on theology. The historical–theological recovery of pure language through sacred texts represents a bulwark against the modern ideology of progress.[62]

In order to achieve these epistemological results, Benjamin undertakes a radical revision of history-writing: "To write history means giving dates their physiognomy."[63] In place of the standard notion of history as pinpointing the dates of events, Benjamin fleshes out the dates themselves, conforming them to a physical image of the body and thus blurring the boundary between text and life. "Giving dates their physiognomy" naturalizes dates and imposes a synchronic structure on them.[64] Instead of supporting chronological history, which in the forms of historicism and the ideology of progress lays claim to objectivity, Benjamin proposes a synchronic and anti-objectivist notion of history-writing:

> The events surrounding the historian and in which he takes part will underlie his presentation like a text written in invisible ink. The history that he lays before the reader will, as it were, shape the quotations in the text, and these quotations alone are put forward in a fashion readable to anybody and everybody. To write history therefore means to *quote* history. But the concept of quotation implies that any given historical object must be ripped out of its context.[65]

History writing is a hermeneutical enterprise that reflects the historian's situation, even in the arrangement of quotations.[66] Nevertheless, decontextualized quotations preserve the accessibility and integrity of historical objects. The task of history-writing—to recover repressed history and to oppose the ideology of progress—is achieved through a montage of quotations: "Method of this project: literary montage. I need say nothing. Only exhibit *(zeigen)*. . . .Only the trivia, the trash—which I don't want to inventory, but simply allow it to come into its own in the only way possible: by putting it to use."⁶⁷ The epistemological problem of history becomes the compositional problem of history-writing, a problem not fully resolved but only programmatically sketched out in the mode of the rhetoric of the task. In one fragment, Benjamin describes history-writing as a "commentary on reality" with theology rather than philology as its main discipline *(die Grundwissenschaft)*.⁶⁸ With a "*weak* messianic power" *(eine schwache messianische Kraft)*,⁶⁹ Benjamin's notion of history recapitulates the linguistic theory: the task of history-writing sets a standard toward which innovative compositions aim.

## "On the Concept of History" (1940)

Benjamin's last completed work conflates theology and historical materialism in a concept of history that aims at "a structure whose site is not homogeneous, empty time, but time filled by the presence of the now *(Jetztzeit)*."⁷⁰ Against historicism and the notions of progress and universal history, historical materialism seeks to "blast open the continuum of history" by the arrest of thought:

> Where thinking suddenly stops in a configuration pregnant with tensions, it gives that configuration a shock, by which it crystallizes into a monad. A historical materialist approaches a historical subject only where he encounters it as a monad. In this structure he recognizes the sign of a Messianic cessation of happening, or, put differently, a revolutionary chance in the fight for the oppressed past.⁷¹

The monad represents a critical stoppage of the forward progress of ordinary thought. The resulting shock signifies both a "Messianic cessation of happening" and "a revolutionary chance in the fight for the oppressed."⁷² The historical materialist arrests the flow of empty time and replaces it with a notion of presentness: "Thus he establishes a conception of the present as the 'time of the now' *(Jetztzeit)* which is shot through with chips of Messianic time."⁷³ Messianic time stands for a full and discontinuous present time that has revolutionary potential as opposed to historicist time, which is empty, continuous, and supportive of the *status quo*.[74]

The essay begins and ends with religious and theological references. At the beginning theology is depicted as a hunchback that operates the automaton of historical materialism but which "today, as we know, is wizened and has to keep out of sight."[75] The image is consistent with Benjamin's understanding of the sacred-profane distinction: the sacred underlies and even constitutes the categories of modern culture, but only indirectly. "In the image of the classless society Marx has secularized the image of messianic time," writes Benjamin in his notes to the essay.[76] Theological and political categories intertwine thoroughly in the text; messianic time functions to recover the politically oppressed past. Like the dual nature of allegorical language, the notion of secular or profane history is understood and constituted by the sacred.[77] This paradox is expressed straightforwardly by Karl Löwith: "Our modern world is worldly and irreligious and yet dependent on the Christian creed from which it is emancipated."[78]

In the final thesis, messianic time is identified with the Jewish conception of history as one that is neither empty (like historicism) nor magical (like that of soothsayers). "We know that the Jews [unlike soothsayers] were prohibited from investigating the future. The Torah and the prayers instruct them in remembrance, however."[79] The result of this remembrance and the messianic hope, Benjamin indicates, is a full notion of history in which "every second of time was the strait gate through which the Messiah might enter."[80] "Messianic time" finds its prototype in the Jewish conception of history.

The momentary nature of true historical understanding appears in several terms frequently used by Benjamin: dialectical image, *Jetztzeit, Augenblick,* and shock. The dialectical image represents a modern form of the emblem in baroque allegory, a visual complex that captures cultural contradictions. Unlike the steady flow of progress characteristic of historicism, the dialectical image captures the true past in an instant: "The true picture of the past flits by. The past can be seized only as an image which flashes up at the instant when it can be recognized and is never seen again".[81]

> Where thought comes to a standstill in a constellation saturated
> with tensions, there appears the dialectical image. It is the cae-
> sura in the movement of thought. Its positioning, of course, is
> in no way arbitrary. In a word, it is to be sought at the point
> where the tension between the dialectical oppositions is greatest.
> The dialectical image ... is identical to the historical object; it
> justifies blasting the latter out of the continuum of history's
> course.[82]

History recovers pure language just as sacred texts do. Epistemo-
logically, the dialectical image induces a stoppage in the flow of
continuous history and provides a critical awareness, if only for
the blink of an eye, of the internal oppositions in history. This is
accomplished on the compositional level through disjointed, aphoristic statements and quotations. As a modern counterpart to the
allegorical emblem, the dialectical image is the historiographic archive of pure language, merging opposites in a dense representation
that yields fleeting insight. The messianic time of *Jetztzeit* is
achieved through the dialectical image; the resulting dialectics at a
standstill stop the continuum of historical progress. Aphorism,
quotation, and the visual images of the chess-playing automaton
and the "Angelus Novus" bring the flow of reading to a stop. The
method of history-writing is also related to storytelling: "The idea
of prose coincides with the messianic idea of universal history.
(Leskov!)"[83] History itself becomes a linguistic phenomenon; like
language, history has fallen and multiplied: "The variety of 'his-
tories' is closely related if not identical with the variety of languages.
Universal history in the contemporary sense is always just a sort
of Esperanto."[84]

"On the Concept of History" criticizes historicism through a
linguistic notion of history. Against the continuity and progress of
prevailing historiography, Benjamin defines history as stoppage and
dialectics at a standstill. This account of history broadens the notion
of sacred text from the Bible and allegory to include the texts of
contemporary literature and history. History reflects a union of
theology and politics, since history represents both the "Messianic
cessation of happening" and "a revolutionary chance in the fight
for the oppressed past."[85] These two functions coincide in the critical

retrieval of memory: "To articulate the past historically does not mean to recognize it 'the way it really was' (Ranke). It means to seize hold of a memory as it flashes up at a moment of danger."[86]

## History and Modernity in the Passagen-Werk (1929–40)

Benjamin intended to implement the philosophy of history in the Arcades project. There, in place of explicitly sacred allegorical texts, the phenomena of early modern culture, ranging from philosophy and literature to architecture and interior furnishings, are analyzed. To account for the simultaneous uniqueness and sameness of modernity, Benjamin views secularization as just another kind of allegorical transformation:

> Pursue the question of whether a link exists between the secularization of time into space and the allegorical perspective. The former, in any case, is hidden in the "worldview of the natural sciences" of the second half of the century, as becomes apparent in Blanqui's last composition. (Secularization of history in Heidegger.)[87]

Blanqui's despairing cosmological text *L'eternité par les astres* mixes theological and astrological accounts of the universe. Although Benjamin shares Blanqui's hellish assessment of modernity, he criticizes his "unrestrained submission" to a scientific model that lacks irony.[88] The natural sciences aim to "secularize" time into space, or in other words, to conform history to the model of space (e.g., linear progress). Even the "world view of the natural sciences," it turns out, represents a modern form of allegory.

The texts and objects of early modern culture represent allegorical transformations of theological categories from earlier periods: "Just as in the seventeenth century allegory becomes the canon of dialectical imagery, so in the nineteenth century does *nouveauté*."[89] Benjamin's earliest notes for the Arcades project include the fragment: "Parallelism between this work and the *Trauerspiel* book: both together the theme: Theology of hell. Allegory[,] advertisement, types: Martyrs, tyrant-whore, speculator."[90]

Adding a new dialectical twist to the observation from the *Trauerspiel* study that allegorical texts simultaneously elevate and devalue language, Benjamin imports allegory to Marx's notion of the commodity fetish: "The devaluation of the world of objects in allegory is outdone within the world of objects itself by the commodity."[91] The chief allegorist of the early modern period is Baudelaire: "It was Baudelaire's endeavour to make the aura which is peculiar to the commodity appear. In a heroic way he sought to humanize the commodity."[92]

Baudelaire's allegories of modern urban experience represent a brilliant but unsuccessful attempt to recover the auratic value of objects, just as the baroque allegory ultimately fails to recover the sacred value of language. The loss of aura in objects, also the subject of the artwork essay, gives rise to the new experience of shock: "He indicated the price for which the sensation of the modern age may be had: the disintegration of the aura in the experience of shock."[93] Shock, which is linked to the concepts of *Jeztzeit* and dialectics at a standstill, represents an allegorical transformation of aura; just as Baudelaire set out to allegorize modern urban experience, shock adopts the epistemological function of aura, which itself has become trivialized and prone to fascism.

A vivid example of the allegorical commodification of objects in modern culture is the souvenir:

> The *souvenir (Das Andenken)* is the relic secularized. The *souvenir* is the complement of the "experience" *(des "Erlebnisses")*. In it the increasing self-alienation of the person who inventories his past as dead possession is distilled. In the 19th century allegory left *(hat geräumt)* the surrounding world, in order to settle in the inner world. The relic derives from the corpse, the souvenir from deceased experience *(Erfahrung)* which calls itself euphemistically *"Erlebnis."*[94]

The analogy is developed later in the manuscript: "The key figure of the early allegory is the corpse. The key figure of the later allegory is the *souvenir.* The *souvenir* is the schema of the transformation of the commodity into a collector's object. The *correspondences* are the endlessly multiple resonances of each *souvenir* with all the others."[95]

The decline of experience[96] and allegory signals the dawn of modernity in the nineteenth century; but these changes only represent new allegorical transformations. Aura gives way to shock, experience is vitiated, and allegory itself becomes internalized. These changes completely alter notions of human nature. The modern hero, for instance, differs from the romantic hero: "The hero is the true subject of modernism. In other words, it takes a heroic constitution to live modernism. . . . With their belief, Balzac and Baudelaire are in opposition to romanticism. They transfigure passions and resolution; the romanticists transfigured renunciation and surrender."[97] Unlike heroes of previous ages, "the modern hero is no hero; he acts heroes. Heroic modernism turns out to be a tragedy in which the hero's part is available."[98] The hero of Baudelaire's poetry allegorically reenacts the tragedy of existing literature; the modern hero only plays the part of hero.

At the same time, modernism exhausts and overwhelms the individual, giving rise to the viability of suicide as an alternative:

> The resistance which modernism offers to the natural productive élan of a person is out of proportion to his strength. It is understandable if a person grows tired and takes refuge in death. Modernism must be under the sign of suicide, an act which seals a heroic will that makes no concessions to a mentality inimical towards this will. This suicide is not a resignation but a heroic passion.[99]

To speak of the "sign" of suicide as an action that "seals" heroism recalls the symbolism and melancholy of baroque allegory. If the modern hero is no hero, then modern suicide is not only suicide but also a sign, an allegorical trope. Benjamin presents the modern suicide as a dialectical image of the contradictions of modernity.[100]

The vast, unfinished *Passagen-Werk* undertakes to revolutionize history-writing and to present a critical history of early modernity. By interpreting the categories of modern experience (such as commodity, shock, and the *flâneur*) as allegorical transformations of earlier religious phenomena, Benjamin's theory of history maintains the persistent importance of sacred text and pure language in modern culture, despite the declining value of experience, the loss of aura in artworks, and the thwarting of the Torah in Kafka. The writings on history and modernity represent more than a melancholy commentary; history-writing is a critical praxis that uncovers and interprets modern culture and leads to a "caesura in the movement of thought." Benjamin's reflections on history offer provisional compositional models (quotation, storytelling, montage) and epistemological categories (shock, profane illumination, dialectics at a standstill) toward this end. The linguistic theory of history takes shape as history-writing, which, like commentary, translation, and philosophy, aims at the restoration of pure language through the biblical concept of sacred text.

## NOTES

1. *GS* 6: 98.
2. See Georgio Agamben, "Language and History in Benjamin," trans. Karen Pinkus, *Differentia* 2 (Spring, 1988): 169–83.
3. *GS*, 5: 1010. Notice the similar formulation of allegory in the *Trauerspiel* study: "The mystical instant *(Nu)* becomes the 'now' *(Jetzt)* of contemporary actuality; the symbolic becomes distorted into the allegorical," *The Origin of German Tragic Drama*, 183.
4. Cf. Adorno's comparison of Benjamin to Kafka:

> But he distinguishes himself from the older Prague writer, who even at times of the most extreme negativity retains an element of the rural, epic tradition, through the far more pronounced moment of urbanity which serves as a contrast to the archaic, and through the resistance to demonic regression acquired by his thought through its affinity to enlightenment, a regression which often leaves Kafka unable to distinguish between the *deus absconditus* and the devil. "A Portrait of Walter Benjamin," in *Prisms*, 235.

5. For Baudelaire, writes Benjamin in the Arcades project, modernity represents not just the "signature of an epoch" but an energy that relates itself to antiquity, *GS* 5: 309.
6. Stéphane Mosès, "The Theological-Political Model of History in the Thought of Walter Benjamin," *History and Memory* 1 (1989): 7.
7. Writing and interpreting texts are central to both Deuteronomy and Benjamin. By broadening the reference of *torah*, the Deuteronomistic redactor inculcates a wide-ranging and reflexive notion of sacred text that makes interpretation necessary. *Torah* becomes life itself for the people, a bold statement collapsing the barrier between the text and life; in fact, Benjamin alludes to Deut. 32:47 in a

letter to Scholem on Kafka *(The Correspondence of Walter Benjamin and Gershom Scholem,* 135). Breadth and reflexivity are thus common characteristics of sacred text in Deuteronomy and in Benjamin.

8. Benjamin, "Central Park," trans. Lloyd Spencer, in *New German Critique* 34 (1985): 32; *GS* 1: 655.

9. *GS* 1: 1239–40, trans. Irving Wohlfarth, "On the Messianic Structure of Walter Benjamin's Last Reflections," in *Glyph* 3 (1978): 172.

10. Wohlfarth, "Messianic Structure," 172.

11. McCole, *Walter Benjamin and the Antinomies of Tradition,* 36.

12. *GS* 2: 16–35.

13. Ibid., 17, 19. Benjamin may have modeled the dialogue on Schopenhauer's "Religion: A Dialogue." In *The Pessimist's Handbook,* trans. T. Bailey Saunders, ed. Hazel E. Barnes (Lincoln: University of Nebraska Press, 1964), 229–74. Perhaps anticipating the position of "the friend," Schopenhauer's Demopheles says, "Religion is the metaphysics of the masses" (Ibid., p. 230).

14. Ibid., 29.

15. Ibid., 28, 34.

16. Ibid., 17.

17. Ibid., 28–29.

18. Ibid., 34.

19. Letter to Ludwig Strauss, September 11, 1912; *GS* 2: 890–92.

20. "Die Religiöse Stellung der Neuen Jugend," *GS* 2: 73.

21. Ibid., 73–74. See McCole's analysis of the essay as an expression of confusion and frustration with the youth movement, p. 58.

22. "Das Leben der Studenten," *GS* 2: 75, translated in McCole, 63.

23. See also "Traumkitsch," *GS* 2: 620–22.

24. "Surrealism," in *Reflections,* 179. The point is elaborated later in the essay: "And it is as magical experiments with words, not as artistic dabbling, that we must understand the passionate phonetic and graphical transformational games that have run through the whole literature of the avant-garde for the past fifteen years, whether it is called Futurism, Dadaism, or Surrealism," ("Surrealism," in *Reflections,* 185).

25. Ibid., 179.

26. Ibid., 189–90.

27. See Adorno, letter to Benjamin, March 18, 1936, in *Aesthetics and Politics,* trans. Harry Zohn (London: Verso, 1977), 120–26.

28. "The Work of Art in the Age of Mechanical Reproduction," 224.

29. Ibid., 231. He continues, "In Western Europe the capitalistic exploitation of the film denies consideration to modern man's legitimate claim to being reproduced," (232).

30. Ibid., 234.

31. "The violation of the masses, whom Fascism, with its *Führer* cult, forces to their knees, has its counterpart in the violation of an apparatus which is pressed into the production of ritual values," (ibid., 241).

32. Ibid., 224 et passim.

33. Ibid., 235–37.

34. Ibid., 222.
35. *Illuminations*, 200, n. 17.
36. *GS* 6: 588.
37. Ibid.
38. "The Storyteller," 83–109; *GS* 2: 438–65.
39. "The Storyteller," in Benjamin, *Illuminations*, 83–84.
40. Ibid., 87–90.
41. Ibid., 84, 90. The link between storytelling and experience recalls the call in "Program of the Coming Philosophy" for a revision of Kant's notion of experience that would include religious categories. Benjamin's choice of Leskov, an explicitly religious writer, as an exemplary storyteller, reflects the importance of religious categories to storytelling and, indirectly, to the revised concept of experience.
42. Ibid., 87. An example of this new beauty is the proverb, which storytelling leaves behind as a remnant: "A proverb, one might say, is a ruin which stands on the site of an old story and in which a moral twines about a happening like ivy around a wall," 108.
43. Ibid., 96, with some changes in the translation.
44. Ibid., 101–2.
45. Ibid., 106.
46. Ibid., 93–94.
47. Ibid., 108–9.
48. See Rudiger Lux, "Der Tod Moses als Ersprochene und Erzählete Welt," *Zeitschrift für Theologie und Kirche* 84 (1987): 395–425. Lux identifies the paradox that in Deut. 32–34, the story of the death of Moses contributes to the "preservation of life in a narrative tradition," 395. Incidentally, this is the only other source known to the author that discusses Deuteronomy 31–34 together with Benjamin.
49. Benjamin, Letter to Scholem, June 12, 1938, in *The Correspondence of Walter Benjamin and Gershom Scholem*, 223. Scholem observes that the identification of mystical experience with tradition alludes to the literal meaning of the Hebrew term *Kabbalah*. The occasion for these reflections is Benjamin's objection to Max Brod's *Kafka*, a book whose attitude of reverent intimacy strikes Benjamin paradoxically as "the most irreverent *(pietätloseste)* attitude imaginable," 220; *Briefe* II, 757.
50. Ibid., 225. An example of this interpretive stance appears in the essay on Kafka: "This village of the Talmud [which represents exile] is right in Kafka's world. For just as K. lives in the village on Castle Hill, modern man lives in his body; the body slips away from him, is hostile toward him. It may happen that a man wakes up one day and finds himself transformed into vermin." "Franz Kafka," *Illuminations*, 126. Benjamin continues, "The air of this village blows about Kafka, and that is why he was not tempted to found a religion"; the statement recognizes the two foci of Kafka's world, since the village refers both to the existing religious world of the Talmud and to the modern world, (ibid). Kafka does not need to create a religion because his work is already religious and because religion becomes problematic in modern experience.
51. Ibid., 129.

52. "Theses," in *Illuminations*, 254, 257–58.

53. Benjamin, Letter to Scholem, August 11, 1934, in *The Correspondence of Walter Benjamin and Gershom Scholem*, 135; *Briefe*, 618.

54. Ibid.

55. "Konvolut N" of the *Passagen-Werk*, "Re The Theory of Knowledge, Theory of Progress," trans. Leigh Hafrey and Richard Sieburth, in *Benjamin: Philosophy, History, Aesthetics*, ed. Gary Smith (Chicago: University of Chicago Press, 1989), 48.

56. Ibid., 72.

57. Ibid., 49–50, 52, 64. The idea of bringing history to a standstill appears much earlier in the romanticism dissertation. See McCole, 108–9. The earliest notes on the Arcades project introduce "dialectics at a standstill" and "dialectical image"; for instance: "Dialektik im Stillstand—das ist die Quintessenz der Methode," *GS* 5: 1035, 1037.

58. Ibid., 67.

59. Ibid., 66.

60. Ibid., 61.

61. Ibid., 47.

62. For a concurring view, see Löwith: "If there is any point where the Greek and the biblical views of history agree with each other, it is in their common freedom from the illusion of progress," *Meaning in History*, 200.

63. "Konvolut N," in *Benjamin: Philosophy, History, Aesthetics*, 67.

64. The blurring of history and nature is also expressed by the notion of "the book of nature," which "indicates that we can read reality like a text. That will be the approach here to the reality of the nineteenth century. We open the book of past events," (ibid., 52).

65. Ibid., 67; notice the persistence of the ink metaphor from the passage quoted above.

66. See Mosès, "The Theological-Political Model of History," 17.

67. "Konvolut N," in *Benjamin: Philosophy, History, Aesthetics*, 47; *GS* 5: 574.

68. *GS* 5: 574.

69. "Theses," in *Illuminations*, 254; *GS* 1: 694.

70. "Theses," in *Illuminations*, 261; *GS* 1: 703.

71. "Theses," in *Illuminations*, 262–63.

72. The concept of the monad is also associated with *Heilsgeschichte*. See *GS* 1: 1234.

73. "Theses," in *Illuminations*, 263.

74. See Wohlfarth, "On the Messianic Structure of Walter Benjamin's Last Reflections." See also Buck-Morss, where the epistemological categories of dialectics at a standstill and *Jetztzeit* are related to messianic time (*The Dialectics of Seeing*, 242–43). Wohlfarth and Buck-Morss tend to schematize the link between political action and messianic reality without recognizing the provisional and compositionally open-ended nature of the "Theses." In my view, the messianic element of history represents a normative horizon rather than an attainable reality, just as pure language is understood in the linguistic theory.

75. "Theses," in *Illuminations*, 253.

76. *GS* 1: 1231.

77. See Ian Balfour, "Reversal, Quotation (Benjamin's History)," in *MLN* 106 (1991): 633.

78. Löwith, *Meaning in History*, 201.

79. "Theses," in *Illuminations*, 264.

80. Ibid. In his notes Benjamin writes that the concept of *Angedenken* (also important in "The Storyteller") is the quintessence of the Jewish notion of history, *GS* 1: 1252.

81. "Theses," in *Illuminations*, 255. See also *GS* 1: 1233.

82. *GS* 5: 595, trans. in Buck-Morss, *The Dialectics of Seeing*, 219.

83. *GS* 1: 1234.

84. Ibid., 1235.

85. "Theses," in *Illuminations*, 263.

86. Ibid., 255.

87. "Konvolut N," in *Benjamin: Philosophy, History, Aesthetics*, 62–63.

88. *GS* 5: 169, trans. in Buck-Morss, *The Dialectics of Seeing*, 106–7.

89. "Paris—the Capital of the Nineteenth Century," trans. Quintin Hoare, in *Charles Baudelaire: A Lyric Poet in the Era of High Capitalism* (London: Verso, 1989), 172.

90. *GS* 5: 1022–23.

91. Benjamin, "Central Park," trans. Lloyd Spencer, *New German Critique* 34 (1985): 34.

92. Ibid., 42.

93. "Some Motifs in Baudelaire," trans. Harry Zohn, in *Charles Baudelaire*, 154.

94. "Central Park," in *New German Critique* 34 (1985): 49; *GS* 1: 681.

95. "Central Park," in *New German Critique* 34 (1985): 55.

96. Recall the central role of recovering *Erfahrung* in the early essay "Über das Programm der kommenden Philosophie," *GS* 2: 157–71.

97. "Paris—The Capital of the Nineteenth Century," in *Charles Baudelaire: A Lyric Poet in the Era of High Capitalism*, 74.

98. Ibid., 97.

99. Ibid., 75.

100. It is therefore ironic that many Benjamin scholars attach decisive significance to Benjamin's own suicide as a motivational key to his philosophy. See Hannah Arendt's Introduction to *Illuminations*, 18; Beth Sharon Ash, "Walter Benjamin: Ethnic Fears, Oedipal Anxieties, Political Consequences," *New German Critique* 48 (1989): 2–42; and Richard Vine, "The Beatification of Walter Benjamin," *The New Criterion* 8 (1990): 37–48.

# Conclusion

$T$his study demonstrates that the idea of sacred text runs through Walter Benjamin's writings. Benjamin's interests in politics, idealism, and religion converged on the Bible. As he experimented restlessly with writing styles, subject matter, and ideology, Benjamin consistently sought discourses that, like the Bible, could help to restore pure language.

Benjamin's interest in the Bible emerged from his search for a critical theory of language. Dissatisfied with Humboldt's view that language reflects thought and serves as a means to ordinary communication, Benjamin developed a model that was both more idealistic and more remote from ordinary experience. The Bible furnished this model: as a sacred text that symbolizes pure language while narrating its loss; an ideal complex that conveys a message; and a supremely translatable revelation that defies comprehension.

Though he was consumed by philosophical problems, Benjamin was always suspicious of their solutions: Kantian philosophy overlooked religion and language, romanticism overconfidently valorized past and future, and political ideologies instrumentalized language. Unlike Buber and Rosenzweig, Benjamin did not think that simply reading the Bible could enlighten modern readers, who see language and the world only through the darkened lens of the Fall; one must first examine that lens. The modern, "profane" forms of art, literature, and commodity culture enabled Benjamin to correlate modernity with pure language, life with Torah.

With more questions than answers and only a weak messianic power, the scholar, critic, and translator turn to texts that perform the scriptural function. Such texts—and the end of Deuteronomy bears this out—portray loss and also permit flashes of critical insight. Their meaning matters less than their manner of expression and their standing in a tradition. This insight led Benjamin to philosophical and compositional experimentation.

As an archive of pure language, Benjamin's sacred text goes beyond the internalist-externalist dichotomy, because it breaks down the distinction between religious and secular cultural forms: philosophy, literature, theology, and even Marxism are imbued with the scriptural function. This tradition is thus always metaphysical, but Benjamin's own metaphysics is characteristically implicit, and it is beyond the scope of this study to spell it out. Following the messianic principle that catastrophe precedes fulfillment, Benjamin devoted much of his energy to the study of failure (e.g., in the *Trauerspiel*) and destructiveness (e.g., Kraus and Baudelaire). This emphasis on absence, loss, and the "infinite task" of philosophy, even while affirming that Torah is life (in Kafka's world at least), suggests a metaphysics of negative messianism.

Benjamin's messianic notions of pure language and sacred text offer critical insight without panaceas. Pure language may not be fully recoverable, but it grants Benjamin the critical leverage to locate and pursue forms of writing that avoid romanticizing or instrumentalizing language. It also suggests some new directions for inquiry in religious studies and critical theory.

The scriptural function illustrates the degree to which Western culture derives from biblical culture. Michel Foucault's analysis of commentary illustrates the hermeneutical influence of sacred text:

> The task of commentary can never, by definition, be completed. And yet commentary is directed entirely towards the enigmatic, murmured element of the language being commented on: it calls into being, below the existing discourse, another discourse that is more fundamental and, as it were, "more primal," which it sets itself the tasks of restoring. There can be no commentary unless, below the language one is reading and deciphering, there runs the sovereignty of an original Text. And it is this text which, by providing a foundation for the commentary, offers its ultimate revelation as the promised reward of commentary.[1]

Foucault's "original Text" overlaps with Benjamin's pure language; both denote a promise that the scriptural function cannot entirely fulfill. The sacred text is not a tangible artifact as much as a form of what Foucault calls "discourse," an identifiable verbal practice that has clear cultural and historical implications. The significance and varieties of commentary on texts in Western culture, and their emergence from the exegetical traditions within and after the Bible, have not been thoroughly explored. The scriptural function encompasses those cultural phenomena that participate in the text-commentary relationship identified by Foucault.

Contemporary hermeneutics also illustrates the role of sacred texts in the study of culture. With Schleiermacher's development of a general hermeneutics out of biblical hermeneutics, interpretive practices previously reserved for the Bible apply to texts in general.[2] Dilthey's hermeneutics of historical *Weltanschauungen* carries the process further, beyond texts into other cultural phenomena. The expansion of hermeneutics is thus a form of secularization, since interpretive methods once reserved for sacred texts are now applied to other phenomena. On the other hand, to the extent that biblical hermeneutics is the basis for general hermeneutics, the scriptural function becomes operative in the study of culture in general.

The biblical concept of sacred text has also shaped the field of religious studies itself. Rudolf Otto's concept of the numinous draws heavily from his understanding of the Bible. *The Idea of the Holy* contains many biblical references and identifies the Hebrew Bible as a *locus classicus* for the numinous, a world where "mystery lives and moves in all its potency."[3] For Otto the progression from the Old Testament to the New Testament forms a master narrative of the progressive rationalization of the numinous and of religion in general.[4] The academic study of religion can thus only be fully understood in light of how the sacred text of the Bible contributes to its conceptual structure.

Theories of interpretation that distinguish between explicit and implicit meaning in texts—psychoanalytic criticism, structuralism, post-structuralism, and feminist hermeneutics—have a basis in the history of biblical interpretation. Freud's interpretations of dreams, Lévi-Strauss's analyses of cultural systems, and Cixous's exposure of how classical thought relates to gender all rely on methods of interpretation and ideas of text in the tradition of the sacred text of the Bible. Such "hermeneutics of suspicion"[5] come full circle when they uncover the scriptural function in contemporary texts that exhibit it only indirectly.

A related area in which the notion of scriptural function can make a significant contribution is the critical theory of communication. Jürgen Habermas's notion of communicative rationality rests on the assumption that "the sacred domain has largely disintegrated, or at least has lost its structure-forming significance."[6] By adopting a Weberian model of secularization, Habermas may be too quick to dismiss the sacred. In fact, it could be argued that communicative rationality participates indirectly in the concept of sacred text, insofar as it depends on the legitimacy and normative value of various modes of interpretation.

Poststructuralism, on the other hand, generally shares an emphasis on texts and intertextuality with the scriptural function.[7] Both positions see Western culture primarily as a set of written traditions. Benjamin's notion of pure language, however, suggests that language is not necessarily the arbitrary free play of signifiers. If poststructuralism claims there is nothing outside the text, Benjamin's philosophy maintains that there may be, despite the degraded condition of language.

Textual interpretation and the status of texts in the West derive largely from the Bible and its history. By recognizing its importance apart from specifics of doctrine and commentary, Benjamin adopted the Bible as a resource for the critique of language and culture. His work demonstrates how the scriptural function has become a form of life, not only for particular religious communities, but for Western culture in general.

## NOTES

1. Michel Foucault, *The Order of Things* (New York: Vintage, 1973), 41.

2. F.D.E. Schleiermacher, *Hermeneutics: The Handwritten Manuscripts,* ed. Heinz Kimmerle, trans. James Duke and Jack Forstman (Atlanta: Scholars Press, 1977), 67–68.

3. Rudolf Otto, *The Idea of the Holy,* trans. John W. Harvey (London: Oxford University Press, 1958), 72.

4. Ibid., 75.

5. Paul Ricoeur, *Freud and Philosophy: An Essay on Interpretation,* trans. Denis Savage (New Haven: Yale University Press, 1970), 32–36, and on the pervasive influence of biblical hermeneutics in Western culture, see 24–25.

6. Jürgen Habermas, *The Theory of Communicative Action,* vol. 2, trans. Thomas McCarthy (Boston: Beacon, 1987), 196.

7. In this context, "poststructuralism" only describes the views I mention, rather than any individual theorist or text.

# The Aura of Benjamin's Death: Interview With Lisa Fittko

The story of Walter Benjamin's death has become almost as well-known as his work; many who have only a passing interest in his philosophy and criticism nevertheless know in some detail how he died.[1] But unlike many other philosophers who died in an untimely or extraordinary way, Benjamin has frequently been identified with the story of his death, and scholars tend to associate the story with his work. Hannah Arendt, for instance, describes Benjamin's death as typical of his entire life: a mixture of his own bungling and an "uncommon stroke of bad luck."[2] It seems that what Benjamin said of Baudelaire applies to himself as well: "The figure of Baudelaire enters in a decisive way into his reputation."[3] In fact, the circumstances of Benjamin's death dramatically overshadow and undermine the serious reception of his work.

These biographically determined interpretations fall into two categories: those that minimize Benjamin's work because of its incompleteness and his untimely (and, it is sometimes added, unnecessary) suicide; and those, on the other hand, that portray Benjamin as a tragic sage whose every utterance was brilliant and quotable but not subject to critical scrutiny. For these writers the death becomes a source of speculation on what Benjamin might have written had he survived. Whether depicting him as a cultic icon or an obscurantist bungler, writings about Benjamin tend to view his work in light of either of these topoi. It is a great irony of Benjamin studies that a thinker who analyzed the abuse of myth and the commodification of modern personae has been reduced to the type of narrative figure he critically studied.

Walter Benjamin's death story does reveal the importance he placed on his writings, even at the risk of his own life. His final actions confirm his own observations on narrative: "Death is the sanction of everything that the storyteller can tell. He has borrowed his authority from death. In other words, it is natural history to which his stories refer back."[4] For many early interpreters of Benjamin—Adorno, Scholem, Arendt, and others—telling Benjamin's story is a way of gaining authority to comment on the meaning of his work, a subject of great contention then and now. Biographical criticism of Benjamin's work tries to impart an aura to the figure of Benjamin, much as film producers in "The Work of Art" essay try to recreate aura around actors with the "cult of the movie star,"[5] in order, it would seem, to keep his work at a distance.

Like the typological allegories of the *Trauerspiel*, the popularity of Benjamin's death story can be explained by its resonance with familiar narrative patterns. For one thing, Benjamin is consistently depicted as a philosopher more at home with his work than in the role of fugitive from the Nazis.[6] He carried texts that he claimed were more important than his own life but which no one has been able to find.[7] He died by taking poison. The circumstances of his death and burial are shrouded in mystery. Two familiar death narratives that resemble and perhaps shape the Benjamin death story are the death of Moses and the death of Socrates. Whereas the Socrates parallels—the voluntary poisoning, the victimization of an uncompromising philosopher—are obvious and compelling, the Moses parallel is also relevant, especially as it relates to the notion of sacred text. The Moses death story reinforces and legitimates Torah, striking a fine balance between life and text, *bios* and *graphé*. The reception of the Benjamin death story, in contrast, tends to focus on the missing texts, the incomplete *Passagen-Werk*, and the unnecessary suicide, thus diminishing the text in favor of biography and overlooking the details of both.

The main source for the story of Benjamin's death is Lisa Fittko, the remarkable woman who led him to the Spanish border in 1940. In *Escape through the Pyrenees*, she describes her experiences as a German Jew in France from 1940 until her escape in 1941. During this time, German refugees were interned by French authorities first as potential enemies and later by the Vichy government to be handed over to the Nazis. While Fittko and her husband, Hans, were waiting for their own escape, they secretly led refugees out of occupied France to safety in Spain. Among them was Walter Benjamin. Her story depicts herself as the opposite of Benjamin in age and temperament, especially with respect to the ability to adapt and improvise under difficult circumstances. She and her husband finally escaped Europe for Cuba in 1941, and today she lives in Chicago's Hyde Park. The story of Benjamin's escape (in a chapter entitled "Old Benjamin") is told with humanity, precision, and humor, without unnecessary sentimentality. In the following interview she elaborates her impressions of Benjamin and the story *behind* the story of Benjamin's death.

## *Abridged Interview with Lisa Fittko*
### *June 27, 1991*

BRIAN BRITT: At the beginning of your piece you say that you always thought of him as "old Benjamin." Why did you think of him as "old Benjamin"?

LISA FITTKO: Well, that's what I asked myself later on. I think I know: I was young, I wasn't a youngster. I was at the end of my 20s and he was, as I later on found out, 48. I never asked about his age; I wasn't interested in it, but he had something aged in his demeanor and appearance. He was a little heavy; he was something of a sage, whatever that means.

BB: So even earlier, even before 1940, you had that impression of him.

LF: I had that impression of him. I was of course speaking in German then, but for some reason I always referred to him as "good old Benjamin." I can't really tell you exactly why. It was just an impression—there was good old Benjamin. He wasn't a close friend of ours. You want to know how I saw him in Paris. He was one of the hundreds of writers and artists who had fled Germany and were, as we saw it, the cream of intellectual and artistic Germany. And they were all running around Paris trying to create a work and make a living, and Paris was just overloaded with them, and I personally didn't really care much; we had a lot of things to worry about ourselves and masses of people, what's going to happen and the world's going to fall apart, so ... it just so happened that he lived in the same building as my brother. And much later I asked him, "What do you remember of Benjamin?" and he said that they lived in the same building and they would play chess, and that was the main point of communication. And then he remembered that he was extremely polite, which many weren't.

BB: You capture that very nicely in your piece, even when he drinks the tainted water and then apologizes.

LF: My brother, who was a theoretical physicist, told me, "I remember that Benjamin never failed to ask me about what I was working on at that point, and I would tell him, even though he had really no knowledge about it, and he would ask me intelligent questions about it and he was interested. It wasn't just politeness, he wanted to know what I was working on ... and he always asked me about my work but I never asked him about his work." So this gives you a little picture of Benjamin, what he was like ... but I can't say we knew him.

BB: He was an acquaintance.

LF: He was an acquaintance, and I think in the book it says through all the translations he was an old friend; he wasn't an old friend. We knew him for a while, and as I say in the same building and chess and all that, but he was an acquaintance. Then came this internment when the war broke out, and that's in the story too, that my husband and he happened to be in the same camp.

BB: And it sounds like your husband was helpful to him.

LF: My husband was a very practical person, and he liked Benjamin, but he just felt that he needed help.

BB: In the text you say that your husband told him this was not a good time to quit smoking and that Benjamin's reply was that he found it good to immerse his mind in an effort.

LF: That's right. He said to him, this is so difficult to stop smoking—because you know he was also a user of morphine—it was so difficult it needed his total concentration, and that would take him away from the misery of the camp which otherwise he couldn't bear, and my husband told me that because after the camp he thought, strange guy, so totally the opposite of my husband, who would always feel what is the practical thing to do.

BB: And that also sounds like his behavior during your walk with him.

LF: Yes, he was ten minutes walking and then he didn't say, "I'm tired now"; he looked at his watch and the watch told him it was time to rest.

BB: As you saw him walking, what was your impression of his physical health?

LF: It wasn't too bad, because he never complained and he never did what you for some reason here call *to schlepp,* he didn't do that; he walked slowly and then he stopped and he said, "Here now my watch tells me now I have to stop for five minutes to regain energy." But he never complained except this one time when he said he couldn't make it up there. And you know when you're young you're very different in that you don't really feel what old or not-so-well people feel. . . . No, he wasn't made to climb the Pyrenees, but my personal impression at that time was that the road wasn't difficult for me, and I didn't really have the impression that it was overstepping his capabilities, but that might have been my perspective as a young person for whom this was easy. And I had a certain amount of anxiety, but I have to say that Scholem, who described it after I described it to him, really went wrong there. He misunderstood or misinterpreted what I was saying about the anxiety. For instance, when he insisted spending the night at that clearing, Scholem, who again was double as old as I, probably saw it from his perspective and he thought I was afraid of the crossing, and maybe we'd be caught and all that; and that was totally far from any of my thoughts. I was scared what this crazy guy was going to do. Crazy guy, you understand how I mean it, you know, staying at night in the mountains where he's never been before, and who knows what's going to happen. I wrote down that little scene where I warned him about the bulls and he was making fun of me.

BB: Yes, he asked, "Are you going to defend me against them?"

LF: Which of course was a bit funny. I was a little girl and he was this man and I understood of course the humor of it. He had a sense of humor, I don't know if anybody ever said that.

BB: Not very much. He once told Scholem that he thought there was a lot of humor in Kafka and that somebody should write about it, but not many people have.

LF: They don't . . . but I had a very strong impression of the replies he gave me; they were very humorous.

BB: Were you quite surprised that he had taken his life?

LF: Was I surprised? It was a total surprise. See, I've answered that question before—what was your impression? People usually ask me, "Weren't you devastated?" To that I have to go back again to the context of the situation. People were committing suicide left and right and it was part of this horrible situation and I certainly was deeply moved, particularly because I had made an effort and I was so happy to have gotten him across, but I cannot say that it hit me the way it would hit me today, because that's what was happening in the world at that time.

BB: Yes, I got the sense from the way you write that that was a very different time and that it's almost impossible to imagine, at least for me, what it was like to live then.

LF: That's the advantage of some people who are alive at my age, they're the only people who can really relive that situation in that context and there are a lot of researchers, I mean historians, and they're digging out a lot of very true and interesting and valuable material, but what it really was like to live through it and the atmosphere and how I'm thinking and feeling I never get from those historians. And I guess I can't expect it.

BB: It's perhaps easier to convey through impressions than through facts and dates.

LF: Well as you know that was the style I chose; I'm not a historian.

BB: It also makes you present as a storyteller; you create an interesting atmosphere of narration.

LF: Actually when the book was first published in Germany I remember that the editor-in-chief said to me, "I've never been as much in a scene as much as I was on the mountain with you and Benjamin, the way you described it." And from that point I felt I better go ahead and write some more.

BB: It's true; everyone I talk to is aware of the story either through your book or through hearing about your telling of it, and considers it very compelling. When you say you were trying to work on that style, what do you mean?

LF: That I was trying and it was very difficult not to bring in today's perspective, not to bring in anything from the forty to fifty years that followed as perhaps exaggerated imagination; to write it the way that I felt it that way at that time, and that might have been totally wrong but I didn't care about that. There were a few reviews that were saying, well, but she must know better now, but that's just what I did not want to put in; I wanted to give a picture because I felt that that was historically also important, a picture of how *we* felt, and this goes through the whole book as I tried to do it.

BB: When I ask were you surprised, I'm wondering what your impression of his mood or his demeanor was during the trip itself. It sounds as if he was able to make one or two slightly humorous statements and that he was very polite.

LF: Well the impression I had of that whole day actually I spent with him—excursion if you want to call it—he certainly wasn't frightened as far as I could tell, he wasn't nervous as far as I could tell, there was only one thing that made me uncomfortable which was, and I don't know if I can explain it well, this man is not really connnected with reality, or as I tried to say at the end of this chapter, his reality is not our reality. And from that I did not conclude he's going to commit suicide—that isn't it—but is he going to take the right—for me the right road—when in danger, when in a situation where he has to make a decision. This was my very stong impression, that he might not judge situations the way I would say normal people would judge.

BB: He didn't have that strong practical sense; you use the French term *débrouillard.*

LF: He was no *débrouillard.* You have to be sly and you have to be out for yourself, and all this was just totally alien to him. I don't know, I never had any reason to think of suicide, except that his priorities were being set so that I thought that this might be very dangerous for him, like for instance remember when he was drinking from this puddle, when he explained to me in his weird way that it's okay that he dies of typhus ... and from these things I got the feeling that this person might not know how to handle situations, and as he did not handle himself I would almost say to him to save himself was to commit suicide. ... That option to him through all the logic, to him the option he had—unjustifiably, but that's beside the point—was to be taken back to France. So to him the rational thing to do was to commit suicide. I don't know, it's difficult for me to tell what was going on in a person like him, but to me this was the logic in which he was working; and there is of course the secret of the manuscript which he obviously felt is in good hands but it was not.

BB: What's your impression of how people react when they hear this story?

LF: Well frankly I have to say among Americans I feel a tendency to sentimentalize it, and to attempt to build it up, I cannot say to more than it is, because the story in itself stands, but to blow it up so that it really becomes sensational, and I have a repulsion against that, because here's this old Benjamin trudging along and we were joking and he wanted a carrot, I'm not minimizing the tragedy of it, but I have an objection to people who make out of it a sensation, which I encounter: "Oh my gosh, the poor guy," and there were so many poor guys. Now Benjamin, from everything I hear from people like you, was one of the greatest guys, and I believe that, but they get too much of a wrong perspective which bothers me just because I'm so close to it; he was a human being and he was a strange human being to me.

BB: In what sense was he a bungler, as you say in the story?

LF: Bungler—I mean in the sense for instance that he didn't know how to hold a tin cup, but I mean it also in a deeper sense, staying alone in the middle of the mountains, because his logic tells him, and this is something that Hannah Arendt was working on too, how he was ... really bungling ... to us ... and I'm just very tentatively putting at the end the argument that for him it wasn't bungling because his reality just wasn't ours. That's what I meant when I said when he was bungling and yet he thought everything through like with this five minute business, he told me that during the middle of the night alone in the mountains since he wasn't afraid. There really were bulls; I didn't make them up, and I was scared of that.

BB: Did you ever feel as if you could persuade him to be more practical or resourceful?

LF: I would say I learned in these one-and-a-half days that I was with him in this situation, I thought, Well he's a normal person, he's at least normal in intelligence I thought, so I can convince him. But in those days I learned that I couldn't convince this man of anything, that I might as well give up, you know the scene later on when we come to this dirty watery thing that he wanted to drink and did drink; I wasn't able to convince this man of anything, and if I had crossed into Spain with them, which I just couldn't do of course ... I wouldn't have been able to convince him that this was not the last word and let's see what happens tomorrow and I'll talk to so-and-so and what not. I think I would not have been able to convince him at all, I think he would have commited suicide; there's one thing I feel very strongly, the suicide he committed was well thought out and I'm not saying he thought about it way before, that I don't know. But many suicides are made out to be from an involuntary mood. That wasn't the case with him at all; he had figured it out, he had calculated everything and that was his way out.

BB: If it was well thought out what do you think his idea was?

LF: Before Benjamin left Paris because of the German invasion he gave his manuscript to Georges Bataille, asking him to hide it in the Bibliothèque Nationale.... He had one copy of that manuscript and that was in that black briefcase ... and he assumed the only existing copy was in that briefcase; he, Benjamin, assumed that the original had fallen in the hands of the Germans and therefore the one goal in his life was to save that manuscript, which he said was his last, and if possible also to save himself, but the manuscript really was of more importance, which might be strange to you but that was just the kind of man he was. There was no doubt about it, there was no maybe about it, and as he explained in that water thing, OK, I might get typhoid fever, I might even die of it, but the Gestapo is not going to get me or the manuscript. And this is where I think the plan of committing suicide if such and such happened was already ripe in him.

BB: And the issue of the manuscript didn't really arise until 1980?

LF: There's a very strange story connected with that. They did find him in the death register, incidentally strangely enough the only one in this whole register whose picture is in, nobody knows how that came together, and then it listed what was found, and it said a black briefcase, and that was the first time [they believed her story] and a pile of papers of unknown contents. Now this was in Catalonia where the language is Catalan, and that was a German manuscript, so I understand why it's of unknown contents, and the thing I want to tell you is, when Horkheimer died, people went through his papers and there was a letter from the magister or whatever you call him from Port Bou; Horkheimer had written to him and had gotten an answer and there was a copy of it and it said again that there was a manuscript, and Horkheimer did not tell anybody and nobody ever knew about that letter until after his death when the letter was found among his papers. Now I'm not going to give you any explanation about that; I'm just giving you facts. But I do know that he was aware that there was a manuscript at the border and he never either told anybody or went for it.

BB: That's very interesting.

LF: Yeah, it's like a *Kriminalroman*, you know.

NOTES

1. An earlier version of this interview appears in *Continuum* 2 (1993): 368–76.

2. *Illuminations*, 18. Other studies significantly shaped by the story of Benjamin's death include Robert Alter, *Necessary Angels* (Cambridge: Harvard University Press, 1991); Beth Sharon Ash, "Walter Benjamin: Ethnic Fears, Oedipal Anxieties, Political Consequences," *New German Critique* 48 (1989): 2–42; Gers-

hom Scholem, "Walter Benjamin and His Angel," *Denver Quarterly* 9 (1974): 1–43; and Richard Vine, "The Beatification of Walter Benjamin," *The New Criterion* 8 (1990): 37–48.

3. "Central Park," 137.

4. "The Storyteller," 94.

5. "The Work of Art," 231.

6. "What a remarkable man! I thought. Crystal-clear thinking, an unfaltering inner strength, and at the same time a hopelessly awkward, clumsy fellow." Lisa Fittko, "Old Benjamin," *Escape through the Pyrenees* (Evanston: Northwestern University Press, 1991): 109.

7. Fittko concludes, "The manuscript could not be found . . . Only the black leather briefcase was entered in the death register back then, with the notation: *unos papeles mas de contenido desconicido*—with papers of unknown content," Fittko, 115. For Fittko's conclusion that the papers were probably only a copy of the "Theses," see the interview.

# Index